KEON LINDSEY

Have You Heard From God Lately?

30 Messages from Heaven to You

Contents

Foreword

During the failed lunar landing attempt of Apollo 13, an oxygen tank aboard the spacecraft blew up, destroying another oxygen tank. When astronaut Jim Lovell looked out the window, he saw their precious oxygen supply "venting" out into space. The lives of three American astronauts hung in the balance. With their ship crippled near the moon, they would have to rely on their Aquarius lunar capsule to return home, but it was not designed to do so.

At the start of all the trouble, commander John L. Swigert Jr. uttered those now famous words: "Okay, Houston, we've had a problem here."

Fortunately, communication between the Apollo 13 crew and engineers at NASA was *not* a problem. Help back in Houston was able to calm fears and give essential guidance through many life-threatening complications aboard Aquarius and bring the three astronauts safely home.

I share this incident because it reminds me of what is happening today, only in reverse. The human race is on Earth in a life and death situation, and time is running out. God in Heaven has sent the life-saving messages we need to rescue us in any plight. Our sufficient help is found in God's Word, the Bible. You and I should be saying daily, "Heaven, we've got a problem here." Then we need to search the Scriptures for God's messages to us.

In his book, *Have You Heard from God Lately?*, Author Keon Lindsey shares *30 Messages from Heaven to You*. He reminds readers of the unlimited power and wisdom of the One sending the messages. Those who follow what God has said will reap the blessings of eternal salvation and lasting change. Each section concludes with questions to make you think about God's message and how it applies to your life. May this book help you develop the spiritual discipline of hearing from God's Word and doing what He has spoken (Matthew 7:24).

Mike Ascher, Senior Pastor
Good News Baptist Church

Introduction – How Does God Speak?

God, who at various times and in various ways spoke in time past to the fathers by the prophets. (Hebrews 1:1)

God spoke in ancient times through various ways. He chose when and how:

- With dreams (Genesis 28:12–16)
- In visions (Ezekiel 1:1)
- By angels (Genesis 19:1)
- As a man (Genesis 18:1–2)
- Through prophets (1 Samuel 15:1–3)

You may also remember that the Lord spoke to Moses from the burning bush (Exodus 3:2–6). These are instances where God spoke specifically to certain people. Of course, God has spoken generally to all mankind through the creation.

The heavens declare the glory of God;
And the firmament shows His handiwork.
Day unto day utters speech,
And night unto night reveals knowledge.
There is no speech nor language
Where their voice is not heard.
Their line has gone out through all the earth,
And their words to the end of the world. (Psalm 19:1–4)

The heavens and sky, even day and night speak. Yes, their words describe God's power and glory to everyone on the planet. Why?

> **Because what may be known of God is manifest in them, for God has shown it to them. For since the creation of the world His invisible attributes are clearly seen, being understood by the things that are made, even His eternal power and Godhead, so that they are without excuse. (Romans 1:19-20)**

Every person knows that God exists from seeing His work in the creation around us. Some acknowledge Him and some do not, but the Lord gives His general revelation or knowledge to all. Through this gift, everyone may desire the specific messages that He has given to each of us.

All the methods and messages were meant to get us ready for the ultimate messenger, Jesus. Therefore, God

> **has in these last days spoken to us by His Son. (Hebrews 1:2a)**

Since Jesus is the supreme messenger, do you think we should pay attention to what He has said? How should we respond? If He is the greatest, should we listen to anyone that contradicts Him? These are critical questions each person needs to consider in order to have a truly fulfilling life. Let's keep these in mind as we look at some messages from Heaven and see how they relate to us today. And of course, we will look at the ultimate message!

Terms

If you are new to the Bible, some of the terminology you will encounter may differ in meaning from their common cultural definitions. To avoid confusion, let me share what these words mean in the biblical context:

- *God* – "the creator and sustainer of the universe who has provided humankind with a revelation of Himself through the natural world and through His Son, Jesus Christ."[1]

- *Lord* – title for God. Instead of saying "the Lord God," we'll use either Lord or God.
- *LORD* – special Hebrew name for God, capitalized in English Bibles to distinguish from the title Lord.
- *Christian* – a believer in Jesus Christ and active follower of His teachings. Not to be confused with the cultural use of the term to describe a westerner who is not Jewish or Muslim.

Also, you will notice sometimes pronouns or other words are capitalized even when they are not the first word of a sentence. These instances indicate a reference to God or something specially related to Him, such as "His Word."

Finally, when citing something from the Bible, the name of the book, chapter, and verse will be given in the text as (Book Name #:#) for easy reference.

---

[1] *Nelson's New Illustrated Bible Dictionary*, p.501, Robert F. Youngblood, Thomas Nelson Publishers 1995.

Message 1 – I Made You for a Purpose

For by Him all things were created that are in heaven and that are on earth, visible and invisible, whether thrones or dominions or principalities or powers. All things were created through Him and for Him. (Colossians 1:16)

Why did God make you? He made you for Him! This is very important because it means you are special and have a purpose. (The Bible tells us in Genesis 2 about the original job and plan God gave to mankind, but we will discuss that in the next message.) You are not a meaningless accident, nor the result of random time and chance. You have worth because the Lord thought you were worth making! Think about that. Since you are worth something, what are you doing with your valuable life? What should you be doing with it?

Therefore, whether you eat or drink, or whatever you do, do all to the glory of God. (1 Corinthians 10:31)

Why Live for God?

Whatever you do with your valuable life, do it to bring glory to God. In modern times, we don't fully grasp the concept of working or fighting for the honor of a superior or ideal. We may get glimpses of it in books or movies when a hero does something "in the name of the king" or when athletes work

1

together for a team victory. However, we often go about our days focused on ourselves, even though science has shown that people who live for something bigger than themselves have happier lives.[2] God says live for Him! He is the greatest cause to whom anyone could be devoted. Living for the Lord brings satisfaction, as one writer declared:

> *Oh, that men would give thanks to the LORD for His goodness,*
> *And for His wonderful works to the children of men!*
> *For He satisfies the longing soul,*
> *And fills the hungry soul with goodness. (Psalm 107:8–9)*

Living for the Lord also brings rewards.

> *But without faith it is impossible to please Him, for he who comes*
> *to God must believe that He is, and that He is a rewarder of those*
> *who diligently seek Him. (Hebrews 11:6)*

Seeking the Lord brings rewards, and He satisfies the soul. This is very encouraging information, but why should we glorify God? Not only because He made us, but also because of His great love for us.

> *But God demonstrates His own love toward us, in that while we*
> *were still sinners, Christ died for us. (Romans 5:8)*

While we were God's enemies, rebels, and sinners, He showed incredible love for us. People are kind and loving towards friends and family. We may even help a stranger. Yet, who loves an enemy so much they would die to rescue the offender? No one but God! You might say, "I was never God's enemy;

---

[2] Various, such as: "The Secret to Happiness Is Helping Others" by Jenny Santi, https://time.com/collection/guide-to-happiness/4070299/secret-to-happiness/ accessed June 9, 2020 and "Happiness Comes from Giving, Not Buying and Having" by Steve Taylor Ph.D. https://www.psychologytoday.com/us/blog/out-the-darkness/201501/happiness-comes-giving-not-buying-and-having accessed June 9, 2020.

how does this apply to me?" We will investigate that question in message two.

This love is beyond human logic and requires a response. If you accept this undeserved love, you should love in return. We should devote ourselves to the Lord and glorify Him in response to His amazing love for us.

We love Him because He first loved us. (1 John 4:19)

The Meaning of Life

God made us for a purpose, but what is it? To discover the meaning of life, let's begin with God's plan for the universe.

[God] having made known to us the mystery of His will...that in the dispensation of the fullness of the times He might gather together in one all things in Christ, both which are in heaven and which are on earth—in Him. (Ephesians 1:9–10)

Did you notice that God's will, which was a mystery, has been revealed? That is, the Lord does not want us to be ignorant of His plans and purposes. This is a wonderful thought—the almighty Creator wants us to know what He is doing! That's why He gave us these messages from Heaven. God's plan is to bring all things, both in Heaven and on Earth, together under the rule of Jesus. This will bring the Lord the glory He deserves. We are told

that at the name of Jesus every knee should bow, of those in heaven, and of those on earth, and of those under the earth, and that every tongue should confess that Jesus Christ is Lord, to the glory of God the Father. (Philippians 2:10–11)

So, the purpose of the universe is to bring God glory. This will happen at the end of time; in the meantime, what does that mean for us today?

3

That we who first trusted in Christ should be to the praise of His glory. (Ephesians 1:12)

Our purpose today is to bring glory to Jesus. This is the meaning of life. It is in this pursuit that we find meaning and lasting satisfaction, and we have a promise that people who are faithful to Jesus will be rewarded. He said,

"When the Son of Man comes in His glory, and all the holy angels with Him, then He will sit on the throne of His glory. All the nations will be gathered before Him, and He will separate them one from another, as a shepherd divides his sheep from the goats. And He will set the sheep on His right hand, but the goats on the left. Then the King will say to those on His right hand, 'Come, you blessed of My Father, inherit the kingdom prepared for you from the foundation of the world: for I was hungry and you gave Me food; I was thirsty and you gave Me drink; I was a stranger and you took Me in; I was naked and you clothed Me; I was sick and you visited Me; I was in prison and you came to Me.' Then the righteous will answer Him, saying, 'Lord, when did we see You hungry and feed You, or thirsty and give You drink? When did we see You a stranger and take You in, or naked and clothe You? Or when did we see You sick, or in prison, and come to You?' And the King will answer and say to them, 'Assuredly, I say to you, inasmuch as you did it to one of the least of these My brethren, you did it to Me.'" (Matthew 25:31–40)

The faithful will "inherit the kingdom." How are we to be faithful? We saw that showing compassion is one way, but Jesus summarized things with the two great commands.

Jesus said to him, "You shall love the Lord your God with all your heart, with all your soul, and with all your mind.' This is the first and great commandment. And the second is like it: 'You shall love

4

your neighbor as yourself." (Matthew 22:37–39)

The first commandment is to love God with everything in you. Make Him your priority; be faithful and devoted to Him. When you do, it will be easier to obey the second command to love others just like you love yourself. Caring for others, showing kindness and compassion brings glory to God and the blessing of fulfillment to us. Please notice that the Lord did not command everyone to be a monk or a nun. Loving Him and our neighbors is what we are to do wherever we are and whatever our vocation may be. So, you can keep these commandments today!

<u>Think About It</u>

1. Do you have worth because of your skills or accomplishments? Where does your worth come from?

2. What is God's plan for the universe?

3. What is God's purpose for you? And how do you fulfill it?

Message 2 – You Ran from Me

Now that we know we were made for God, what about the garden of Eden and His original plan for mankind? Why aren't we in paradise now?

> *Then God said, "Let Us make man in Our image, according to Our likeness; let them have dominion over the fish of the sea, over the birds of the air, and over the cattle, over all the earth and over every creeping thing that creeps on the earth." (Genesis 1:26)*

God designed mankind to rule the Earth for Him. He had a specific job for the first man, Adam, and gave him a home in the famous garden of Eden.

> *Then the LORD God took the man and put him in the garden of Eden to tend and keep it. And the LORD God commanded the man, saying, "Of every tree of the garden you may freely eat; but of the tree of the knowledge of good and evil you shall not eat, for in the day that you eat of it you shall surely die." (Genesis 2:15–17)*

The Lord wanted Adam to take care of the garden. Adam could enjoy all the benefits of living there, including the fruit. There was just one rule—but why should paradise have any rules at all? Why did God put something in the garden that man could not have?

Is God Unfair?

Some might say it was unfair of the Lord to put Adam in that situation. However, that is not fair to God. Why do parents make rules for their kids? In order to keep them safe. Yet we look at God like small children look at their parents. They say to themselves, "That hot stove won't burn me. It's a fun toy that they don't want me to enjoy!" Humanity exhibits this same childish attitude toward God's rules. As adults, we should know better. After all, we understand that not only does a stove pose a danger when used improperly, it has a purpose. If we remove them from houses so kids would have no risk of a burn, no one could cook healthy meals. Since the danger must remain in place, so must the boundaries.

Just as many things that are off limits to kids have a purpose greater than they can grasp, the forbidden fruit also had a purpose. Although God made us for Himself, He did not force us to be for Him. Our Creator wants us to choose Him so we can have a real relationship. Thus, the fruit that was off limits allowed Adam to decide whether he wanted to be for God or not.

It also made Adam think. Should he trust God? His Creator gave him life, a home, a job, and put him in charge of the planet. Would Adam be satisfied with all that power and responsibility, or would he grasp for more and risk the consequences of disobeying? Did he want to be in charge of the universe and take God's job?

So, you see, the forbidden fruit had nothing to do with God holding out on Adam or being unfair, as some people mistakenly believe. It was about the Creator letting the creature choose who would be his God. Today we have to make the same choice. Will we submit to our Creator's authority and enjoy His blessings? Or do we want to play god and make our own rules? What did Adam do? He listened to the voice that said, "Don't believe God."

Then the serpent said to the woman, "You will not surely die. For

God knows that in the day you eat of it your eyes will be opened, and you will be like God, knowing good and evil."

So when the woman saw that the tree was good for food, that it was pleasant to the eyes, and a tree desirable to make one wise, she took of its fruit and ate. She also gave to her husband with her, and he ate. (Genesis 3:4–6)

Most people wrongly blame Eve, the first woman, for eating the forbidden fruit. Yes, she made a terrible choice, but the Bible clearly says that Adam was with her. He was there and was tempted right beside Eve. Adam made the decision to be his own god, and in doing so he turned away from the Lord.

And they heard the sound of the LORD God walking in the garden in the cool of the day, and Adam and his wife hid themselves from the presence of the LORD God among the trees of the garden. (Genesis 3:8)

When the real God showed up, Adam literally ran away. However, in his heart, he had already run when he decided to disobey.

What does this mean for us? Since Adam was our first father, he represented us to the Lord, just as a king or president represents a nation to the world. If the national head starts a war, the people of that nation are implicated in the decision and impacted by the results. That's how things work, whether we like it or not.

Thus, when Adam ran away from the Lord, we ran with him. Most people will scream, "That's not fair. I would not have eaten the forbidden fruit!" Yet, in reality, we make the same choice Adam and Eve did every day. We want to be our own god. Even though we are born away from the Lord because of Adam's sin, it is our choice if we go back or stay away.

God Calls Us to Choose

"I call heaven and earth as witnesses today against you, that I have set before you life and death, blessing and cursing; therefore choose life, that both you and your descendants may live." (Deuteronomy 30:19)

Over and over again, the Lord tells us that we can choose Him. (For example, see Joshua 24:15, 1 Kings 18:21, and Proverbs 1:20–23.) Choose to submit to God's rule instead of your own and enjoy His blessings.

What happens if we choose to stay away or keep running away from God? The Lord told Adam he would die if he ate the forbidden fruit (Genesis 2:17). Adam was supposed to live in his body forever, but he began to die when he disobeyed.

Then to Adam He said, "Because you have heeded the voice of your wife, and have eaten from the tree of which I commanded you, saying, 'You shall not eat of it':
"Cursed is the ground for your sake;
In toil you shall eat of it
All the days of your life.
Both thorns and thistles it shall bring forth for you,
And you shall eat the herb of the field.
In the sweat of your face you shall eat bread
Till you return to the ground,
For out of it you were taken;
For dust you are,
And to dust you shall return." (Genesis 3:17–19)

Before Adam died physically, he would experience pain and suffering from the curse of rejecting God. We also experience pain and suffering as a consequence of running from the Lord. However, worse than physical pain and death is the spiritual death of being separated from God forever in the lake of fire.

> *"But the cowardly, unbelieving, abominable, murderers, sexually immoral, sorcerers, idolaters, and all liars shall have their part in the lake which burns with fire and brimstone, which is the second death." (Revelation 21:8)*

This second death, which is the reward of sin (Romans 6:23), is worse than terrible. Thankfully, the Lord did not leave us hopelessly lost away from Him. We will see in the next message that He wants us back!

Think About It

1. Why is it easier to blame God for rules than it is to see a good purpose behind them?

2. Why do we want to be our own gods rather than submit to the Lord's authority?

3. Why is it unwise to run from the Lord?

Message 3 – I Want You Back

Humanity is like an unfaithful spouse cheating on God. We think the excitement of new pleasure abroad is better than the safety and security of a true loving relationship at home. In fact, the Lord used this very illustration numerous times in the Bible.

> *For your Maker is your husband,*
> *The LORD of hosts is His name. (Isaiah 54:5a)*

Our Creator made us for a wonderful relationship with Him. We left, and we suffer as a result. Yet the Lord is not content to leave us in our misery.

> *The Lord is not slack concerning His promise, as some count slackness, but is longsuffering toward us, not willing that any should perish but that all should come to repentance. (2 Peter 3:9)*

God does not want us to die as sinners and suffer, separated from Him for eternity. Even as judgment was pronounced on Adam and Eve for the first sin, there was also a promise. The Lord would send someone to fight and defeat Satan, the enemy who wants to keep humanity from God (Genesis 3:15).

You may ask, "Why didn't God defeat Satan immediately when he tempted Adam and Eve?" If He did, would Adam and Eve have had an opportunity to choose God? Or would they have realized what life was like without God?

This is an important question for us today as well. Consider what the Lord said about Israel when they ran from Him.

> *"For their mother has played the harlot;*
> *She who conceived them has behaved shamefully.*
> *For she said, 'I will go after my lovers,*
> *Who give me my bread and my water,*
> *My wool and my linen,*
> *My oil and my drink.'*
> *Therefore, behold,*
> *I will hedge up your way with thorns,*
> *And wall her in,*
> *So that she cannot find her paths.*
> *She will chase her lovers,*
> *But not overtake them;*
> *Yes, she will seek them, but not find them.*
> *Then she will say,*
> **'I will go and return to my first husband,**
> **For then it was better for me than now.'"** *(Hosea 2:5–7*
> *emphasis added)*

God allows and even brings struggles to get people to realize that with Him "it was better for me than now." Individually, when we suffer and have pain, it should make us realize that life without the Lord is miserable! The fact that misery continues in spite of our best efforts to be good or to achieve higher status should let us know that we cannot save ourselves. Further, all our efforts to reform society, bring peace, and usher in utopia with education, government, and science fail as well. These sad realities tell us that, individually and collectively, we need a Savior!

The Lord used the life of the prophet Hosea to illustrate this concept for us. His wife literally ran away after lovers. The wife had sold herself into sin, so it would cost Hosea to get her back (Hosea 3:2). God talked with Hosea about this terrible situation.

> *Then the LORD said to me, "Go again, love a woman who is loved by a lover and is committing adultery, just like the love of the LORD for the children of Israel, who look to other gods and love the raisin cakes of the pagans." (Hosea 3:1)*

God told Hosea to rescue his cheating wife and show love to her that she did not deserve. He was to demonstrate God's love for people who ran from their Creator.

Real Love

The Lord's love is not like human love. Our love is a changing emotion. God's love is permanent. That doesn't mean He cannot be disappointed or get upset. It means He does what is best for us, even if it hurts. It is a sacrificial commitment.

> *"For God so loved the world that He gave His only begotten Son, that whoever believes in Him should not perish but have everlasting life." (John 3:16)*

God's love for humanity, including you, is so great that He sent His Son Jesus to save us from sin and death. This cost more than we can imagine. To accomplish the rescue, Jesus had to live a perfect life on Earth and die to pay for our sin.

> *For as by one man's disobedience many were made sinners, so also by one Man's obedience many will be made righteous. (Romans 5:19)*

Adam's disobedience made us all sinners, because we inherited a sinful nature

13

from our ancestor. Yet Jesus' righteousness can pass to us as well because He obeyed perfectly for us. Now, whenever a person "believes in Him," they get eternal life. This is great news, but how does it happen?

But as many as received Him, to them He gave the right to become children of God, to those who believe in His name. (John 1:12)

When we trust Jesus as our Savior—that is, place our faith in Him to bring us to God—we are adopted into His family. As sons and daughters of God, we regain the right standing with the Lord that we lost from being born as descendants of Adam.

Think About It

1. Why didn't the Lord fix Adam's sin problem immediately?

2. Despite humanity's best efforts at reform, we are still miserable. What does this tell us?

3. How much does God love you?

Message 4 – You Can't Live Without Me

We previously mentioned that the Lord lets us choose how we live, with or without Him. So, what did society look like in the early years after mankind first ran away from the Creator?

> *And Cain knew his wife, and she conceived and bore Enoch. And he built a city, and called the name of the city after the name of his son—Enoch...*
>
> *And Adah bore Jabal. He was the father of those who dwell in tents and have livestock. His brother's name was Jubal. He was the father of all those who play the harp and flute. And as for Zillah, she also bore Tubal-Cain, an instructor of every craftsman in bronze and iron. (Genesis 4:17, 20–22)*

Early man used God-given skills to develop technology and build a society without the Lord. Did you notice they did not live in caves, but in cities and tents? Cities, or even a village, cannot exist without a social structure and division of labor. At a minimum there must be farmers and builders. Yet they had metal workers, indicating a high degree of specialization and technological progress. The ancient civilization even had musicians, which means they had time for hobbies and recreation.

How Bad?

These results don't seem too bad for living without God, do they? In fact, it's rather like civilization today. We are technologically advanced with instant information, prepackaged food, specialized careers, and free time for entertainment. Where is the negative part of all this?

Then the LORD saw that the wickedness of man was great in the earth, and that every intent of the thoughts of his heart was only evil continually. (Genesis 6:5)

That sounds really bad! Mankind was not just wicked, they were *greatly* wicked! The word wickedness in the original language means "evil" and came from a word meaning broken and good for nothing.[3] In spite of their technological achievements, they had a broken and worthless society.

Additionally, the individuals only thought about evil all day long! Is that even possible, to never have a good thought? Think about Joseph Stalin, Adolf Hitler, and Osama Bin Laden—what happens when there's only evil on the inside? It comes out.

The earth also was corrupt before God, and the earth was filled with violence. (Genesis 6:11)

The world was corrupt or ruined. Furthermore, it was filled with violence. Early man had a terrible life in spite of science and technology. How would you like to live in a war zone, or maybe a neighborhood dominated by lawless gangs, with violence everywhere?

This is the result of building a life or society without God. You can achieve high levels of technology and even cultural arts, but the unrestrained evil inside will ruin everything and make life wretchedly miserable. Our society today almost looks like this, but the evil inside the modern man has some restraint that the first civilization did not have. What happened?

---

3 *Strong's Exhaustive Concordance of the Bible*, Hebrew definition 7451, Hendrickson Publishers.

A Second Chance

That first civilization was judged by the famous worldwide flood that Noah survived (Genesis 6:13, 7:17–24). After the flood, when Noah came off the ark, the Lord gave mankind a fresh start with the institution of government. God said,

> *"Whoever sheds man's blood,*
>   *By man his blood shall be shed;*
> *For in the image of God*
> *He made man." (Genesis 9:6)*

Mankind could no longer run wild like a rabid dog attacking or killing whenever they wanted. Since the human conscience had failed to restrain the evil inside, the Lord instituted government to be an external restraint. It is obvious that God will hold everyone accountable in the afterlife, but in the meantime, if you hurt someone, you will be held accountable on Earth by fellow humans. The Lord has even given earthly authorities the power to execute murderers.

> *For rulers are not a terror to good works, but to evil. Do you want to be unafraid of the authority? Do what is good, and you will have praise from the same. For he is God's minister to you for good. But if you do evil, be afraid; for he does not bear the sword in vain; for he is God's minister, an avenger to execute wrath on him who practices evil. Therefore you must be subject, not only because of wrath but also for conscience' sake. (Romans 13:3–5)*

Before the flood, there was no government to protect the innocent and condemn the guilty. Now there is. Though we still have criminally immoral and irrational actors in our society, most people's evil intentions are restrained by fear of the law. You might not like paying taxes, but you should thank God for government; without it, your life would be terrible and come to an early, violent end. Thus, government lets us live long enough to come to our senses and run back to God. Even though mankind still resists the Lord, our Creator is gracious and has not left us hopeless to our own devices. We cannot live without Him, even with our best efforts.

Think About It

1. How is it that people can rebel against God yet accomplish their goals? (Hint: who gives talents?)

2. Can any of these accomplishments last? Why or why not?

3. Why did the Lord give us government?

Message 5 – Rules Are Good for You

We saw that the Lord was merciful when He gave government to humanity. Knowing our sinful hearts could and would abuse government, He also gave rules for our good. Since God's rules are supreme, human rules are subject to them as well (Acts 5:29). What were the first rules, and how are they good?

> *"But you shall not eat flesh with its life, that is, its blood. Surely for your lifeblood I will demand a reckoning; from the hand of every beast I will require it, and from the hand of man. From the hand of every man's brother I will require the life of man." (Genesis 9:4–5)*

The first rules concern blood. Humans were allowed to eat meat, but only once its blood had been drained; it could not be eaten raw. Matthew Henry explained in his famous commentary that this showed "that though they were lords of the creatures, yet they were subject to their Creator, and under the restraints of His law."[4]

Blood is life; it is not to be eaten. In modern times, we know that blood carries disease (as do other bodily fluids), so we can see God's protection for early man. Besides this, blood belongs to God. Later in the Bible, when explaining the law of sacrifices, the Lord said,

---

[4] *Matthew Henry's Commentary on the Whole Bible*, Vol 1, p.57, Hendrickson Publishers, Inc. Peabody Massachusetts, 1991.

"For the life of the flesh is in the blood, and I have given it to you upon the altar to make atonement for your souls; for it is the blood that makes atonement for the soul." (Leviticus 17:11)

We will explore this more later, but for now remember that blood and life belong to God. The other rule about blood is that murderers must be executed for their crime. God is the owner of life, and He does not permit you to take another person's life just because you want to. Obviously, this rule is highly beneficial to mankind.

Famous Rules

God's most famous rules are the Ten Commandments. Why were they given? God said,

"Now therefore, if you will indeed obey My voice and keep My covenant, then you shall be a special treasure to Me above all people; for all the earth is Mine. And you shall be to Me a kingdom of priests and a holy nation." (Exodus 19:5–6a)

When the Lord rescued the Israelites from slavery in Egypt, they had not been faithfully living for Him. So, God gave laws to teach them how to be His people and to show others how to approach the Creator. The first laws He passed down to them are known as the Ten Commandments, and they were divided into two sections.

Commandments one through four taught how people were to relate to God. Moses recorded,

And God spoke all these words, saying:
"I am the LORD your God, who brought you out of the land of Egypt, out of the house of bondage.
"You shall have no other gods before Me.

"You shall not make for yourself a carved image...you shall not bow down to them nor serve them...
"You shall not take the name of the LORD your God in vain, for the LORD will not hold him guiltless who takes His name in vain.
"Remember the Sabbath day, to keep it holy." (Exodus 20:1–8)

Notice that before giving any rules, God laid out the basis of His authority over them. He had shown great power in rescuing the people from bondage; therefore, they were to be loyal and only worship the Lord. These first four commandments bring blessings to us as well by putting us in good relationship with our Creator.

Commandments five through ten taught how to relate to other humans. God said,

"Honor your father and your mother, that your days may be long upon the land which the LORD your God is giving you.
"You shall not murder.
"You shall not commit adultery.
"You shall not steal.
"You shall not bear false witness against your neighbor.
"You shall not covet...anything that is your neighbor's." (Exodus 20:12–17)

Instructions for relating to people begin in the home. In learning to honor our parents, we learn how to submit to proper authority and show respect for others. Then we recognize rights to life, marriage, property, and the value of truth in protecting those rights. Finally, in the command not to crave what others have, we learn to be content. When we are content, we have no motivation to harm others. We appreciate what God has given and can live in an orderly society.

The Problem with Rules

These laws allow for and enforce peace on planet Earth. The Lord in His wisdom gave them to protect us and to allow all people to flourish. God's law is good, and we should obey it. The problem is that we can't obey all the rules all the time because we still have our internal problem of sin.

> *For whoever shall keep the whole law, and yet stumble in one point, he is guilty of all. (James 2:10)*

One slip up and we are condemned. So, what good is the external law?

> *Is the law then against the promises of God? Certainly not! For if there had been a law given which could have given life, truly righteousness would have been by the law...*
>
> *Therefore the law was our tutor to bring us to Christ, that we might be justified by faith. (Galatians 3:21, 24)*

The law was like a teacher helping us understand what perfect righteousness looks like. With our eyes open to how far short we fall of that standard, we realize our need for someone to be perfect for us. So, the law points us to Jesus, the one person who was able to follow the law's requirements. God's laws are very good for us!

Think About It

1. Are you the type of person who likes rules or not? Why or why not?

2. Why does God have the right to make rules? Why are human rules to be subject or secondary to His?

3. What are some reasons God's rules are good for us?

Message 6 – I Want to Bless You

From the very beginning, God has been blessing humans.

So God created man in His own image; in the image of God He created him; male and female He created them. Then God blessed them. (Genesis 1:27–28a)

Even before our Creator spoke a blessing, we know He was giving blessings by providing the Earth as a home filled with food and resources for us (Genesis 1:29). God also blessed us with companionship in marriage (Genesis 2:18). Later, when Noah came off the ark, God blessed mankind again (Genesis 9:1). Additionally, in message four we saw how the Lord blessed us with government for our protection, even though we ran away from Him. These are general blessings for humanity, but the Lord has blessings for individuals also.

Specific Blessings for an Individual

Now the LORD had said to Abram:
"Get out of your country,
From your family
And from your father's house,
To a land that I will show you.
I will make you a great nation;
I will bless you

23

> *And make your name great;*
> *And you shall be a blessing.*
> *I will bless those who bless you,*
> *And I will curse him who curses you;*
> *And in you all the families of the earth shall be blessed." (Genesis 12:1–3)*

What do these blessings for Abram (known to us as Abraham) tell us?

1. God has a plan for each of us. Sometimes we must leave our comfort zone to experience His blessings, just as Abram had to leave his hometown.
2. We should not keep or use God's blessings selfishly. Notice the direct link between the Lord blessing Abram and Abram becoming a blessing.
3. God takes care of His own, just as He promised protection for Abram.
4. Abram would bless the whole world.

Each point on this list is remarkable, but the last especially stands out. How could Abram hope to bless the whole world? The Lord would use Abram and his descendants, the people of Israel, to show and tell the world how to come back to God. This was the most important blessing mankind could get after being separated from the Creator. In general, when Israel obeyed the Lord and received earthly blessings, the people around them would notice and inquire about God. For example, when the queen of Sheba saw all of Solomon's blessings, she said,

> *"Blessed be the LORD your God, who delighted in you, setting you on the throne of Israel! Because the LORD has loved Israel forever, therefore He made you king, to do justice and righteousness." (1 Kings 10:9)*

Throughout the Old Testament, there are many examples of people learning about God from Israel. However, the specific blessing promised to Abram for the world is Jesus! The Lord promised to send a Savior for all nations through his family. We will look more in depth at this greatest blessing later. For now, let's look at a few other good things God has for us.

Blessings Available to Everyone

"He makes His sun rise on the evil and on the good, and sends rain on the just and on the unjust." (Matthew 5:45b)

Even though we rebel against God, He still gives sunshine and rain so we can live and grow food.

If any of you lacks wisdom, let him ask of God, who gives to all liberally and without reproach, and it will be given to him. (James 1:5)

God gives wisdom to those who ask for it. It is so important that we are told,

For wisdom is better than rubies,
  And all the things one may desire cannot be compared with her. (Proverbs 8:11)

The Lord's blessings are more valuable than gems. Have you thought about anything worth more than money lately?

Blessed be the God and Father of our Lord Jesus Christ, who has blessed us with every spiritual blessing in the heavenly places in Christ. (Ephesians 1:3)

The Lord has spiritual blessings for those who follow Jesus. Notice that if you get one spiritual blessing, you get all of them. "It is not so with temporal blessings," Matthew Henry tells us in his commentary. "Some are favored with health, and not with riches, some with riches, and not health, etc. but where God blesses with spiritual blessings, He blesses with all."[5]

What are these spiritual blessings? According to Ephesians 1, God chooses us, adopts us as His children, forgives our sins, and gives us His grace. These blessings are quite amazing and last forever!

So, the Lord provides both earthly and spiritual blessings. There are some earthly blessings for all mankind to enjoy, namely creation. Some earthly gifts are measured out here and there; for instance, we have health or wealth to varying degrees. However, these are temporary, so we should not focus too much on them. The spiritual blessings are better. God gives them freely and does not withdraw them. They last forever and are the most valuable.

Think About It

1. When did God begin blessing humans? Has He ever stopped?

2. What are some general blessings available for all mankind? What are some specific blessings that are given by measure?

3. What are the most valuable types of blessings and why?

---

[5] Ibid, Vol 5, p.553.

Message 7 – I Want You to Be Wise

God wants people to be wise-truly wise. Why?

> *For the wisdom of this world is foolishness with God. (1 Corinthians 3:19a)*

Earthly wisdom is actually foolish! How can that be?

> *There is a way that seems right to a man,*
> *But its end is the way of death. (Proverbs 14:12)*

Earthly wisdom is shortsighted. It only looks at the here and now instead of the long-term. Even worse than that, it is selfish and says, "Get all you can, however you can, as fast as you can so that you can be happy, no matter who you hurt in the process." Earthly wisdom teaches, "If it feels good, do it" and "live for the moment," because "you only live once."

Satan used earthly wisdom to tempt Adam and Eve to sin against the Lord. In Genesis 3:1–5, he basically said, "Look at that nice juicy fruit. It looks so good; how can it be bad? It will give you wisdom like God so you can be the boss!" It was pure foolishness to disobey the Lord, especially when the Almighty had said the consequence was death. Yet in their earthly wisdom, Adam and Eve only thought about what they could get, and they ignored what their Creator said.

God doesn't want you to be a fool and ruin your life and future. That's why He gave us the Bible, filled with heavenly wisdom—true wisdom. It is so important that an entire book of the Bible is dedicated to wisdom. From its opening verses, Proverbs urges the reader to seek after wisdom and treasure it:

> *To know wisdom and instruction,*
>   *To perceive the words of understanding,*
>   *To receive the instruction of wisdom,*
>   *Justice, judgment, and equity;*
>   *To give prudence to the simple,*
>   *To the young man [or woman] knowledge and discretion.*
> *(Proverbs 1:2–4)*

Notice that wisdom, instruction, perception, and understanding are linked. You don't get these by accident. Heavenly wisdom is needed for justice, sound judgment, and fairness. Proverbs can give the virtue of prudence to the unlearned and discretion to the young. Yes, God's wisdom is incredibly important for us:

> *Happy is the man who finds wisdom,*
>   *And the man who gains understanding;*
>   *For her proceeds are better than the profits of silver,*
>   *And her gain than fine gold.*
>   *She is more precious than rubies,*
>   *And all the things you may desire cannot compare with her.*
> *(Proverbs 3:13–15)*

Wow, true wisdom is more valuable than gold and jewels. Those who have it are happy. Do you have this wisdom? Let's see some words of wisdom so you can begin to be truly happy.

Words of Wisdom for Living

The fear of the LORD is the beginning of knowledge,
But fools despise wisdom and instruction. (Proverbs 1:7)

Wisdom starts with reverence for the Lord. Remember, He sees all and knows all. When we honor and respect our Creator, we are ready to listen and receive.

Trust in the LORD with all your heart,
And lean not on your own understanding;
In all your ways acknowledge Him,
And He shall direct your paths. (Proverbs 3:5–6)

Trust God more than your own limited insights so He can guide you in the right way. (We would all be happy if Adam and Eve had done this!)

Hear, my children, the instruction of a father,
And give attention to know understanding. (Proverbs 4:1)

Help children learn to listen to parents so they can understand what is important in life.

Do not enter the path of the wicked,
And do not walk in the way of evil. (Proverbs 4:14)

Don't follow the crowd, and stay off the path of evil.

Keep your heart with all diligence,
For out of it spring the issues of life. (Proverbs 4:23)

Guard your heart and mind with everything you've got. Why?

The familiar saying "garbage in, garbage out" puts this proverb in modern terms. If you put worthless, foolish, or dirty things into your mind, that is what will come out in your words and deeds. This is a vital concept to learn if you want to have the blessing of wisdom. Jesus even emphasized this when He said,

> *"How can you, being evil, speak good things? For out of the abundance of the heart the mouth speaks. A good man out of the good treasure of his heart brings forth good things, and an evil man out of the evil treasure brings forth evil things." (Matthew 12:34b–35)*

You can't bring out what you don't have. Therefore, if you want to live wisely and experience the blessings of discretion, you must take time to pursue wisdom and put prudent things into your mind.

Pause and ask yourself, what messages does the music you listen to put into your heart? How about the videos or movies you watch? What about the people you hang out with? Are they pushing you closer to God or away from Him? Are they taking time away from learning the Lord's instructions, or do they speak His words into your life?

Here are a few more words of wisdom to consider.

> *Go to the ant, you sluggard!*
> *Consider her ways and be wise,*
> *Which, having no captain,*
> *Overseer or ruler,*
> *Provides her supplies in the summer,*
> *And gathers her food in the harvest. (Proverbs 6:6–8)*

Don't be lazy and let an ant be smarter than you! Go to work and save up so you'll have provision in lean times.

Whoever commits adultery with a woman lacks understanding;
He who does so destroys his own soul. (Proverbs 6:32)

Sexual sin is not only foolish, but it will destroy you. Our society ignores this truth, causing many to pay a heavy price with broken hearts, homes, and bodies filled with sexually transmitted diseases.

In the multitude of words sin is not lacking,
But he who restrains his lips is wise. (Proverbs 10:19)

Don't talk too much.

When pride comes, then comes shame;
But with the humble is wisdom. (Proverbs 11:2)

Pride leads to shame, mostly because proud people are too stubborn to listen to wise counsel. But the humble are smart enough to listen and enjoy the blessings of wisdom.

As a ring of gold in a swine's snout,
So is a lovely woman who lacks discretion. (Proverbs 11:22)

Beauty without brains or godly discernment is out of place. Value your mind and right thinking before trying to impress others with how you look.

Fools mock at sin. (Proverbs 14:9a)

Fools laugh at sin. Please, don't be a fool!

<u>Think About It</u>

1. What are some problems with earthly wisdom? What does it focus on?

2. Why is true wisdom, or heavenly wisdom, so important?

3. In what areas of your life do you need to apply heavenly wisdom? Did any of the examples in Proverbs stand out to you?

There is much more to see and learn from Proverbs. Take time to read from this book each day.

Message 8 – I Want to Take Care of You

A surprising number of Bible passages compare people to sheep. We think of sheep as cute, cuddly cotton balls as seen in cartoons. However, sheep are not pretty, nor strong, nor are they smart. They are helpless and completely dependent upon a shepherd. The shepherd must protect the flock because sheep can't defend themselves. He must lead them to grass and water or they will get lost. You may recall from the message on wisdom,

> *There is a way that seems right to a man,*
> *But its end is the way of death. (Proverbs 14:12)*

People get lost trying to make their own way, thus sheep are a good representation. This is why the prophet said,

> *All we like sheep have gone astray;*
> *We have turned, every one, to his own way. (Isaiah 53:6a)*

We want to do our own thing and find our own way, so we wander off the right path. We walk into danger without realizing it. That is why Jesus said,

> *"I am the good shepherd. The good shepherd gives His life for the sheep." (John 10:11)*

The Good Shepherd

A good shepherd cares for his sheep. That is, he provides and protects. He defends against thieves and wild animals, even to the point of death. Jesus wants to be our shepherd and care for us, so we can say,

> *The LORD is my shepherd;*
> *I shall not want. (Psalm 23:1)*

Sheep who follow the Good Shepherd don't have to worry about anything. Why? He knows the big picture of times and seasons. He knows the lay of the land. He will get the flock to the place of food and shelter. Jesus even told us why we do not need to worry.

> *"Look at the birds of the air, for they neither sow nor reap nor gather into barns; yet your heavenly Father feeds them. Are you not of more value than they?*
> *Therefore do not worry, saying, 'What shall we eat?' or 'What shall we drink?' or 'What shall we wear?' For after all these things the Gentiles seek. For your heavenly Father knows that you need all these things. But seek first the kingdom of God and His righteousness, and all these things shall be added to you." (Matthew 6:26, 31–33)*

If God takes care of the birds, won't He take care of you, who are worth far more? We don't have to worry about life. If we seek the Lord—that is, if we follow the Good Shepherd He sent—He will take care of us.

A word of caution: this message is not saying you don't have to work or plan for the future. Rather, instead of worrying, trust Jesus and follow Him. When sheep follow the shepherd to the meadow, they still must chew the grass.

He makes me to lie down in green pastures;
  He leads me beside the still waters.
  He restores my soul;
  He leads me in the paths of righteousness
  For His name's sake. (Psalm 23:2–3)

Jesus leads to the place of nourishment and refreshment. His way is the path of righteousness, where blessings are found. Yet He does not promise all sunshine and no rain.

Yea, though I walk through the valley of the shadow of death,
  I will fear no evil;
  For You are with me;
  Your rod and Your staff, they comfort me. (Psalm 23:4)

Sometimes the shepherd must lead us through dark and scary places. He does not do this to frighten us, but because something good waits for us on the other side. The challenges, trials, and heartaches of life are made bearable by the presence of the Good Shepherd. Difficulty and danger are never fun, but we don't have to fear because the Good Shepherd is standing guard with His rod and staff.

For He Himself has said, "I will never leave you nor forsake you."
(Hebrews 13:5b)

Even when enemies arise, God cares. He provides so that you may have fullness in spite of opposition.

You prepare a table before me in the presence of my enemies;
  You anoint my head with oil;
  My cup runs over.
  Surely goodness and mercy shall follow me
  All the days of my life;

35

And I will dwell in the house of the LORD forever. (Psalm 23:5–6)

We can trust that God's goodness and mercy will be with us all our days because we know where the Good Shepherd is taking us. He cares for the sheep as He leads from blessing to valley, all the way to Heaven, the house of the Lord. Is Jesus your shepherd? Are you following Him today?

Think About It

1. Why do we need a shepherd? Why do we need God to care for us?

2. A shepherd provides and protects. How does the Good Shepherd provide for and protect His people?

3. What is the Good Shepherd's ultimate destination for the sheep? Does knowing the destination help with the difficult parts of the journey?

Message 9 – I Want You in Heaven

Remember, we were made to be with God. He wants us to be in His family on Earth so we can live in His home in Heaven. That is why He sent Jesus, who said,

> *"In My Father's house are many mansions [dwelling places]; if it were not so, I would have told you. I go to prepare a place for you. And if I go and prepare a place for you, I will come again and receive you to Myself; that where I am, there you may be also."* *(John 14:2–3)*

Did you get that? Jesus is preparing a dwelling place in Heaven for His followers! Why is He doing that? So "that where I am, there you may be also." Jesus wants us to be with Him! This is super exciting and caused the Apostle Peter to praise God for His goodness:

> *Blessed be the God and Father of our Lord Jesus Christ, who according to His abundant mercy has begotten us again to a living hope through the resurrection of Jesus Christ from the dead, to an inheritance incorruptible and undefiled and that does not fade away, reserved in heaven for you. (1 Peter 1:3–4)*

Peter reminds us that the Lord is very merciful. He did not leave us lost in sin, though we ran away. Instead, He sent Jesus, as the Good Shepherd, to seek and rescue us. Through His death and resurrection, we can be born again, not as members of Adam's sinful family, but reborn spiritually into God's holy family. As members, we have a great inheritance in Heaven. This inheritance will not rust, fade, or decay like our earthly treasures. Thankfully, our heavenly treasures last forever.

Since the Lord wants us in Heaven and went through great pains to give us access, how should we live on Earth?

> *Therefore, holy brethren, partakers of the heavenly calling, consider the Apostle and High Priest of our confession, Christ Jesus. (Hebrews 3:1)*

Once you have been reborn into the heavenly family, you are a holy brother or sister. Therefore, consider Jesus. That means, think about Him, listen to Him, follow His example, and orient your everyday life with Heaven in mind.

> *"Do not lay up for yourselves treasures on earth, where moth and rust destroy and where thieves break in and steal; but lay up for yourselves treasures in heaven, where neither moth nor rust destroys and where thieves do not break in and steal. For where your treasure is, there your heart will be also." (Matthew 6:19–21)*

When you seek heavenly treasure instead of earthly riches, your heart and priorities can focus on what is truly important. This will help you to live expectantly,

> *looking for the blessed hope and glorious appearing of our great God and Savior Jesus Christ. (Titus 2:13)*

When we live for Jesus, we can look joyfully forward to seeing Him in glory. Additionally, we can expect a good reward on judgment day.

"For the Son of Man will come in the glory of His Father with His angels, and then He will reward each according to his works." (Matthew 16:27)

Rewards in Heaven

God has promised rewards in Heaven to the faithful. Consider these examples:

Finally, there is laid up for me the crown of righteousness, which the Lord, the righteous Judge, will give to me on that Day, and not to me only but also to all who have loved His appearing. (2 Timothy 4:8)

Blessed is the man who endures temptation; for when he has been approved, he will receive the crown of life which the Lord has promised to those who love Him. (James 1:12)

And when the Chief Shepherd appears, you will receive the crown of glory that does not fade away. (1 Peter 5:4)

Can you imagine the Creator of the universe giving crowns to mere humans? He will also grant rest from labor (Hebrews 4:9) and comfort.

And God will wipe away every tear from their eyes; there shall be no more death, nor sorrow, nor crying. There shall be no more pain, for the former things have passed away. (Revelation 21:4)

No more crying, sickness, or pain. In fact, we will get amazing new bodies.

For our citizenship is in heaven, from which we also eagerly wait for the Savior, the Lord Jesus Christ, who will transform our lowly body that it may be conformed to His glorious body, according to

the working by which He is able even to subdue all things to Himself.
(Philippians 3:20–21)

You may have heard the term "glorified body" before. That concept comes from this promise of a new body like the one Jesus has. Such bodies will match our status as citizens of Heaven. These are just a few of the promises that prove God wants you in Heaven!

Heaven or Hell?

The Lord is not slack concerning His promise, as some count slackness, but is longsuffering toward us, not willing that any should perish but that all should come to repentance. (2 Peter 3:9)

The Lord has clearly said that He does not want anyone to perish on judgment day. This is why He is patient and gives us time to repent—to turn away from sin and turn to Jesus. If God did not want you in Heaven, He would have zapped you after your first sin and not given a chance to repent.

Consider the case of Nebuchadnezzar, the evil Babylonian king. This man was cruel, unstable, selfish, and proud, and he warred against nations just because he wanted to. He was like the Hitler of the ancient world; we might look at his actions and think it would have been better if God zapped him early in life. Yet, in the book of Daniel, chapters 1–4, history records that God gave Nebuchadnezzar warnings and help multiple times so he would repent. Eventually, he did and gave a wonderful testimony of how great God is (Daniel 4:37). Read the exciting story for yourself and see just how much the Lord cares for us, even if we are rotten sinners. Why is this so critical? Because, as Jesus warned us, the judgment day is coming.

"When the Son of Man comes in His glory, and all the holy angels with Him, then He will sit on the throne of His glory. All the nations will be gathered before Him, and He will separate them

one from another, as a shepherd divides his sheep from the goats...
Then the King will say to those on His right hand, 'Come, you
blessed of My Father, inherit the kingdom prepared for you from
the foundation of the world...'
    "Then He will also say to those on the left hand, 'Depart from
Me, you cursed, into the everlasting fire prepared for the devil and
his angels.'" (Matthew 25:31–32, 34, 41)

One day Jesus will return to judge the world. Notice He did not say "if" but "when." This is 100 percent certain. Jesus will sit on His throne of glory and divide saints from sinners. To the saints He will say, "Welcome, Heaven is your home." To the sinners He will say, "Depart from My presence; your home is the lake of fire."

Also, please realize who the everlasting fire was prepared for: the devil and his demons. God never intended for any human to go to Hell. As we have seen, He doesn't want any of us there. Yet, it is our choice. Will you follow Jesus to Heaven, or will you follow Satan to Hell?

Think About It

1. Why do you think God wants you in Heaven? (Hint: John 3:16)

2. The best thing about Heaven will be being with God. Yet, He tells us there will be additional benefits. What are some of the other blessings in Heaven?

3. Why is it critical for people to prepare for Heaven now, rather than later? (Hint: Do we know on what day will judgment come?)

Message 10 – You Can't Earn Heaven

We have seen that God really wants us in Heaven and went through a lot of trouble to get us there. Why would the Almighty have to work to get us to Heaven? Shouldn't we work to earn it? Think back to the lost sheep that we discussed:

> *All we like sheep have gone astray;*
> *We have turned, every one, to his own way. (Isaiah 53:6a)*

We previously demonstrated how humans ran away from God and every one of us is like a lost sheep. We know that sheep are helpless. They can't find anything. No matter how hard they try, lost sheep will remain lost.

However, we don't like to think of ourselves as helpless, so we look to human wisdom that says, "Be good and you will get to Heaven." Is that true? After all, Jesus said,

> *"You have heard that it was said, 'You shall love your neighbor and hate your enemy.' But I say to you, love your enemies, bless those who curse you, do good to those who hate you, and pray for those who spitefully use you and persecute you, that you may be sons of your Father in heaven... For if you [only] love those who love you, what reward have you? ...Therefore you shall be perfect, just as your Father in heaven is perfect." (Matthew 5:43–48)*

Notice that Jesus said perfect people, not merely good ones, go to Heaven. Are you perfect? Can you be perfect? No, it is not possible. Recall this passage from message five:

> *For whoever shall keep the whole law, and yet stumble in one point, he is guilty of all. (James 2:10)*

It's Not Fair!

It only takes one sin to make you imperfect. Once you do it, you cannot undo it. That single choice will keep you out of Heaven. You may say, "That's not fair! What if my good deeds outweigh my bad deeds?" We imagine that being as good as possible should be good enough. And most of the religions that have risen to prominence across human history affirm that idea:

- Do all the rituals to please the gods and they will take care of you.
- Be good in this life and you'll have it good in the next life.

How will you know when you have been good enough? Who sets the standard for Heaven? The humans who invented these religious systems have not been to Heaven, nor have they come from Heaven! Therefore, religion cannot be relied upon to protect one's soul. In fact, this idea is a cruel trick of the devil. Just like he tricked Adam and Eve, he wants us to depend on ourselves. If we believe our own efforts can earn Heaven, we will miss it!

The truth is, like the lost sheep, we can never find our way. Believing that we can is the height of pride, and pride is a terrible sin.

> *Everyone proud in heart is an abomination to the LORD; Though they join forces, none will go unpunished. (Proverbs 16:5)*

Pride is so bad it is an abomination, a word defined by *Nelson's New Illustrated*

Bible Dictionary as "'impure,' 'filthy,' 'unclean'—that which is foul-smelling and objectionable to a holy God."[6] Pride is so gross to God that He finds it sickening. Do you think the holy Lord will let anything unholy and sickening into His house?

Hard Facts

Humility is the cure for pride. Once we realize the true extent of our sinfulness, we will see that our pride is unjustified and seek God's help. So here is the truth about us without Jesus, given as a dose of humility.

> *What then? Are we better than they? Not at all. For we have previously charged both Jews and Greeks [non-Jews] that they are all under sin.*
> *As it is written:*
> *"There is none righteous, no, not one;*
> *There is none who understands;*
> *There is none who seeks after God.*
> *They have all turned aside;*
> *They have together become unprofitable;*
> *There is none who does good, no, not one."*
> *"Their throat is an open tomb;*
> *With their tongues they have practiced deceit";*
> *"The poison of asps is under their lips";*
> *"Whose mouth is full of cursing and bitterness."*
> *"Their feet are swift to shed blood;*
> *Destruction and misery are in their ways;*
> *And the way of peace they have not known."*
> *"There is no fear of God before their eyes." (Romans 3:9–18)*

This is a horrible picture! Would you want anyone fitting this description to

---

[6] Youngblood, p.8.

be your friend? Does this describe you? In reality, no matter how good we think we are, this is how we look to a perfect and holy God. When we try to earn our way to Heaven by doing good, we come as dirty, contaminated people offering dirty, contaminated gifts to Someone who hates filth and contamination.

> *But we are all like an unclean thing,*
>   *And all our righteousnesses are like filthy rags. (Isaiah 64:6a)*

Now can you see why it is foolish to think we can earn Heaven?

You may ask, "Why should I bother being good or nice or obey the law if these things will not get me into Heaven?" We are to be good and obey laws so that society will work and we don't kill each other. You might recall we discussed this in messages four and five. Keeping rules is good for your safety and has nothing to do with going to Heaven.

Here is another way to look at it: The sin that keeps us out of Heaven is like a deadly contagious disease. If God let you into Heaven, it would become contaminated and would no longer be paradise. So, you must be cured before you can enter. However, you cannot cure yourself. You need a specialized doctor with specialized medicine. Being nice will not cure the disease. Giving to charity will not fix it. Obeying the law won't help. Paying your taxes won't solve the problem. We need to do all these things, but they cannot get rid of the disease of sin. So, what hope do we have? We must come to God for the cure.

> *"Come now, and let us reason together,"*
>   *Says the LORD,*
>   *"Though your sins are like scarlet,*
>   *They shall be as white as snow;*
>   *Though they are red like crimson,*
>   *They shall be as wool." (Isaiah 1:18)*

45

The Lord said He can cure our deadly disease of sin. However, it must be on His terms and His way—only in humility can we "reason together" as instructed here. We will find out how later.

Think About It

1. What keeps us out of Heaven?

2. Why can't good works or being nice get us into Heaven?

3. Who knows the way to Heaven? (Hint: He lives there.)

Message 11 – You Must Trust Me

Now that it is clear we could never earn Heaven by doing good, how do we get in? Do we need to discover something like a divine nature inside ourselves? Do we need to be enlightened? Can we meditate our way to Heaven? These thoughts require trusting in one's self to find the answer and are really just an internal way of trying to earn Heaven. If we cannot earn Heaven by external action, why should we think it could be done by internal action either? Consider what Jesus said:

> *"For a good tree does not bear bad fruit, nor does a bad tree bear good fruit. For every tree is known by its own fruit. For men do not gather figs from thorns, nor do they gather grapes from a bramble bush." (Luke 6:43–44)*

Trees produce fruit according to their nature. Apple trees make apples. Do you think an apple tree could make figs by deciding to look within? No! You cannot get figs from an apple tree because it has only apples in its genes. So, too, we who are sinners by nature cannot think the sin out of ourselves, nor through mental discipline become saints worthy of Heaven.

> *"But those things which proceed out of the mouth come from the heart, and they defile a man. For out of the heart proceed evil thoughts, murders, adulteries, fornications, thefts, false witness, blasphemies. These are the things which defile a man." (Matthew 15:18–20a)*

It is important to understand that the definition of who we are is fully separate from what we do. We are defined by who we are on the inside. If you want goodness inside yourself, you need a good heart. However, we are born with evil hearts that separate us from the Lord. Romans 3:9–18, which we examined in message ten, describes our terribly corrupt state.

Friend, it is sad to say, but if a human looks inside himself for salvation, he will stay lost (Proverbs 14:12). Our internal compass is broken and no amount of staring at it or meditating or trying to get in touch with an inner being will ever fix it!

> *A fool has no delight in understanding,*
> *But in expressing his own heart. (Proverbs 18:2)*

In fact, if you find an inner being, it will be just as corrupt as you! Please don't be the fool trying to find yourself—you are lost! And don't trust someone who offers you a way to Heaven that is not God's way.

> *And He spoke a parable to them: "Can the blind lead the blind?*
> *Will they not both fall into the ditch?" (Luke 6:39)*

According to Jesus, people who don't know the Lord are spiritually blind. They cannot lead you to Heaven.

Your Way or God's Way?

Jesus said,

> *"Enter by the narrow gate; for wide is the gate and broad is the*
> *way that leads to destruction, and there are many who go in by it.*
> *Because narrow is the gate and difficult is the way which leads to*
> *life, and there are few who find it." (Matthew 7:13–14)*

There are only two ways in life—the way to Heaven and the way to Hell. Many people foolishly think there are many paths to Heaven because they are on the broad, easy road. The people who spread this faulty logic have not been to Heaven, are spiritually blind, and stubbornly trust in their corrupt nature to uncorrupt itself.

God is the only one who knows the way to Heaven. It is His home, so we must trust Him instead of ourselves to get there. He sent messengers like prophets and angels in ancient times to tell mankind, "Listen to the Lord and trust Him." Finally, He sent one Man from Heaven to confirm that message and show us how to get to Heaven (John 6:38). That man is Jesus, and He has firsthand knowledge because Heaven is His home. In the quote above, He said there are only two paths in life. One way that leads to Heaven, and the broad way, which, though wide enough to look like many paths, goes one direction—to Hell. Why do so many people take the broader road? They trust themselves.

He who trusts in his own heart is a fool. (Proverbs 28:26a)

God warned us over and over again: do not trust your corrupt heart! Instead,

Trust in the LORD with all your heart,
   And lean not on your own understanding;
   In all your ways acknowledge Him,
   And He shall direct your paths. (Proverbs 3:5–6)

Trust the Lord. He knows what you do not. He can see what you cannot. Commit your heart to Him and He will put you on the right path.

Why Can We Trust God?

With all we have seen so far, it is obvious we should trust God. Yet why wasn't it obvious before? Most of us create a false image of God in our mind based on what we see or want rather than based on who He said He is. Often, we think of the Creator as a genie in a bottle waiting to grant us wishes if rubbed the right way. Or we think He is a grandfather in a rocking chair; nice enough, but unable to help in everyday life. Can you see how fitting God into our little deity mold limits His trustworthiness?

However, the Almighty has shown Himself trustworthy and describes Himself as both powerful and concerned.

> *Have you not known?*
> *Have you not heard?*
> *The everlasting God, the LORD,*
> *The Creator of the ends of the earth,*
> *Neither faints nor is weary.*
> *His understanding is unsearchable. (Isaiah 40:28)*

God is the everlasting Lord! He is the Creator who does not get tired or grow old.

> *God has spoken once,*
> *Twice I have heard this:*
> *That power belongs to God. (Psalm 62:11)*

He has all power and authority in the universe.

> *The eyes of the LORD are in every place,*
> *Keeping watch on the evil and the good. (Proverbs 15:3)*

The Lord sees all things.

> *"Am I a God near at hand," says the LORD,*
> *"And not a God afar off?*
> *Can anyone hide himself in secret places,*

So I shall not see him?" says the LORD;
  "Do I not fill heaven and earth?" says the LORD. (Jeremiah 23:23–24)

God is everywhere.

"Therefore know that the LORD your God, He is God, the faithful God who keeps covenant and mercy for a thousand generations with those who love Him and keep His commandments." (Deuteronomy 7:9)

God's keeps His promises and is faithful.

The LORD has appeared of old to me, saying:
  "Yes, I have loved you with an everlasting love;
  Therefore with lovingkindness I have drawn you." (Jeremiah 31:3)

God is loving.

This almighty, eternal, all-knowing, all-wise, faithful, and loving God is worthy of trust. When He says you can only get to Heaven His way, we must believe it.

Think About It

1. Why can't humans produce a way to Heaven or discover one on their own?

2. Why did God command us to trust Him in Proverbs 3:5–6?

3. What are some reasons the Lord is trustworthy?

Message 12 – I Came to Rescue You

We have seen that though the Lord wants us in Heaven, it is impossible to reach by any form of human effort. How then are we to get in? We learned that trusting God is necessary to get to Heaven, but what does that mean? This is what Jesus came to tell us. He said,

> *"The Son of Man has come to seek and to save that which was lost."*
> *(Luke 19:10)*

God sent Jesus to rescue us. He came to seek and save lost souls and bring them to Heaven. We've discussed how people are like sheep who wandered away and became lost. Jesus is the Good Shepherd that came to rescue the lost sheep. In fact, He gave us this illustration:

> *"What man of you, having a hundred sheep, if he loses one of them, does not leave the ninety-nine in the wilderness, and go after the one which is lost until he finds it? And when he has found it, he lays it on his shoulders, rejoicing. And when he comes home, he calls together his friends and neighbors, saying to them, 'Rejoice with me, for I have found my sheep which was lost!'"* (Luke 15:4–6)

People are happy when they find lost things. Most of us do not have sheep but can imagine the feeling of losing a pet. We would go looking in rain, heat, or cold, asking people in the neighborhood, stopping strangers on the street to ask, "Have you seen…?" When the beloved animal is found, we would be ready to throw a party.

Jesus left the comfort and warmth of Heaven to find us. Can you imagine God humbling Himself to put on a human body? The Creator, whom angels serve, lowered Himself to walk as a man. The holy and righteous One came to live in a spiritually dark, dirty, and cold world to find you. What did He find? Not just a lost sheep wandering in the hills. He found you chained in slavery to sin (2 Timothy 2:26).

> *Jesus answered them, "Most assuredly, I say to you, whoever commits sin is a slave of sin. And a slave does not abide in the house forever, but a son abides forever. Therefore if the Son makes you free, you shall be free indeed." (John 8:34–36)*

As humans, we like to think we're in control. We think we can do what we want or change ourselves when we want. The truth is once we have sinned by breaking God's law, we in essence become addicted to sin. By definition, you can't free yourself from an addiction; you must have outside help. As we have seen, we cannot rescue ourselves; we need someone to rescue us. Jesus is the only one who can break sin's chains on your life. He is the only one who can get you into Heaven.

Jesus Is the Only Rescuer

> *Jesus said to him, "I am the way, the truth, and the life. No one comes to the Father except through Me." (John 14:6)*

This is a bold but true statement. We know entrance into Heaven cannot be achieved by any human effort, whether internal or external. There is no religion that can take you there. So why can Jesus do it?

Remember that if someone was perfect and never sinned, they can go to

53

heaven (Matthew 5:43–48)? Jesus came to live a perfect life in our place and give up that life for us.

> *For as by one man's disobedience many were made sinners, so also by one Man's obedience many will be made righteous. (Romans 5:19)*

We were born sinners because we inherited our ancestor Adam's sin. Consequently, his offense came on all people. Since Jesus is God, He was born into humanity without sin. He was perfectly righteous. Therefore, He could take the penalty for our sin and transfer His righteousness to us.

> *For He made Him who knew no sin to be sin for us, that we might become the righteousness of God in Him. (2 Corinthians 5:21)*

This summarizes the spiritual process of God removing our sin. It began with a physical act.

> *Christ died for our sins according to the Scriptures, and that He was buried, and that He rose again the third day according to the Scriptures. (1 Corinthians 15:3b–4)*

The Bible is clear. Jesus not only died to pay for our sin but came back to life so that we might know He actually has the power to save us.

> *His Son Jesus Christ our Lord...was born of the seed of David according to the flesh, and declared to be the Son of God with power according to the Spirit of holiness, by the resurrection from the dead. (Romans 1:3b–4)*

Jesus' resurrection from the dead is the ultimate proof that He is God and can rescue us. No other human has ever lived or could ever live a perfect life. No other person can pay for your sin. No one else raised Himself from the dead. Jesus did what only God can do, and He had this ability because He is God. He is the only Savior.

Think About It

1. Why do we have joy after finding something that was lost? Do you think there is rejoicing in Heaven when a lost soul is found?

2. What qualified Jesus to rescue us? (Hint: What did He not have?)

3. What is the ultimate evidence that Jesus is God and has the power to save us?

Message 13 – You Must Choose

Hopefully, you have seen how much God loves you in the past few messages. Specifically, how

> *God demonstrates His own love toward us, in that while we were still sinners, Christ died for us. (Romans 5:8)*

God demonstrated incredible love by sending Jesus to rescue you. He did not come because you or any other human were great, mighty, or righteous. On the contrary:

> *For when we were still without strength, in due time Christ died for the ungodly. (Romans 5:6)*

We were weak, hopeless, and sinful. That's why we need rescuing. Jesus' great love for you caused Him to pay a great price for your sin.

> *By this we know love, because He laid down His life for us. (1 John 3:16a)*

Yet it is not God's love that saves you. It is because of His love that He made a way for you to be saved. This is an important distinction. God's love is available to all, yet all do not go to Heaven. Why?

God Will Not Force You into Heaven

"For God so loved the world that He gave His only begotten Son, that whoever believes in Him should not perish but have everlasting life." (John 3:16)

This amazing love requires a choice. God's love does not force you to love Him in return, but invites you to choose Him and His salvation. "Whoever believes" means you can trust Jesus, but you do not have to. From the beginning, the Lord has offered humans a choice. In the garden of Eden, Adam could have chosen to obey and live. Later Moses echoed this choice when he said,

"I call heaven and earth as witnesses today against you, that I have set before you life and death, blessing and cursing; therefore choose life, that both you and your descendants may live; that you may love the LORD your God, that you may obey His voice, and that you may cling to Him, for He is your life..." (Deuteronomy 30:19–20a)

Heaven and Earth bear witness to the fact that the Lord allows us to decide. He has laid out the options: His way, the path of blessing and life; or our way, the path of sin and death. God wants us to love Him, but He will not make us do it. The famous general Joshua repeated Moses' declaration to the people:

"Now therefore, fear the LORD, serve Him in sincerity and in truth...

And if it seems evil to you to serve the LORD, choose for yourselves this day whom you will serve." (Joshua 24:14a, 15a)

These verses make it clear that we must choose whether to live for God or our own desires. This message was a constant theme of God's prophets in ancient times.

And Elijah came to all the people, and said, "How long will you falter between two opinions? If the LORD is God, follow Him; but if Baal, follow him." But the people answered him not a word. (1 Kings 18:21)

You can't have some of God and some of another religion. That is really just rejecting God. In case there was any doubt, Jesus said,

"No one can serve two masters; for either he will hate the one and love the other, or else he will be loyal to the one and despise the other. You cannot serve God and mammon." (Matthew 6:24)

Mammon literally means riches. It could be physical wealth or anything you hope will enrich your life apart from God. Anything that competes with your Creator for your heart. You can only have one master. You must choose whether to commit yourself wholly to God, or not at all. Therefore, the Lord extends an invitation.

Be Reasonable

"Come now, and let us reason together,"
   Says the LORD.
   "Though your sins are like scarlet,
   They shall be as white as snow...
   If you are willing and obedient,
   You shall eat the good of the land." (Isaiah 1:18–19)

God said to come sit down and think things through. Can you imagine the Almighty wanting to pause and help you understand the true meaning of life? It is amazing that He is not too busy for us.

The Lord describes how a person's sins are dark red. We can't change that color, but He can! He can turn the dirty red into a clean, bright white. All we have to do is be willing, to choose to let Him do it. The reasonable choice is to go with God, as we learned in message ten. Jesus reinforced this invitation with another one:

> *"Come to Me, all you who labor and are heavy laden, and I will give you rest. Take My yoke upon you and learn from Me, for I am gentle and lowly in heart, and you will find rest for your souls."* *(Matthew 11:28–29)*

Jesus said, "Come to Me." You are welcome; He wants you. Notice Jesus spoke to our need when He said the phrase, "you who labor." What labor is this? Is it physical work? Jesus does care for workers, but since He is offering rest for your soul, it makes sense that He is referring to people trying to work their way to Heaven.

Sin is a heavy burden on our soul, and we've seen that no matter how hard we try, we cannot get rid of it. We can do all the good deeds in the world; we could meditate 24 hours, seven days a week; but we would only wear ourselves out in a futile effort to be free from sin. Jesus calls us to take His yoke—that is, choose to live under His authority—and we will find it gentle, providing freedom from sin and rest for the weary soul.

Friend, are you tired of the rat race of life? Are you scurrying along trying to avoid problems while pursuing pleasure but never finding satisfaction? Would you rather have peace in your soul? Choose Jesus.

Maybe you're looking for more than this world offers. If so, look here:

> *Jesus stood and cried out, saying, "If anyone thirsts, let him come to Me and drink. He who believes in Me, as the Scripture has said, out of his heart will flow rivers of living water." (John 7:37b–38)*

Deep down, we know there's more to life than a job, a car, a house, or a party.

Are you thirsting for something to satisfy your soul? Jesus invites you to come and receive lasting satisfaction.

"Whoever drinks of the water that I shall give him will never thirst. But the water that I shall give him will become in him a fountain of water springing up into everlasting life." (John 4:14)

He will give you the living water your soul needs. Jesus doesn't give just a little; He will fill you to overflowing. What could be more gratifying than having your soul's need met and receiving an abundant blessing that you can share with others? Are you thirsty? Come to Jesus. Admit your sin and shortcomings, ask Him to rescue you, and trust Him to do it.

Think About It

1. Why does God offer us a choice instead of forcing us to do what He wants?

2. Why should you choose Jesus?

3. What might hold you back from choosing Jesus? In the grand scheme of life, is it worth it to reject God?

If you want to choose Jesus, and need more information on exactly what to do, turn to the appendix in the back of this book titled, "How to Get to Heaven."

Message 14 – I Am King

We have talked quite a bit about what God does and desires, including how He wants a relationship with us. Yet we have not talked much about who He is. Who is God?

> *The LORD is King forever and ever. (Psalm 10:16a)*

God is the everlasting King, but king over what?

> *For the kingdom is the LORD's,*
> *And He rules over the nations. (Psalm 22:28)*

The Lord is king over all nations. Yet if God is a deity, should He reign only over mankind?

> *For the LORD is the great God,*
> *And the great King above all gods. (Psalm 95:3)*

The Lord is God. He rules over spirits as well as humans. Why is God king?

> *The earth is the LORD's, and all its fullness,*
> *The world and those who dwell therein. (Psalm 24:1)*

The Earth belongs to God. All creatures are His by divine right. Why?

In the beginning God created the heavens and the earth. (Genesis 1:1)

God made everything. The universe is His by right of creation.

Authority

What are the implications of being part of God's creation and not just a randomly occurring accident of nature? You'll recall from the first message that you have worth because you were made for a purpose. Also, God's status as Creator means that He gets to make the rules—and He can delegate authority to others. We see such an example in our secular society:

> *Let every soul be subject to the governing authorities. For there is no authority except from God, and the authorities that exist are appointed by God. Therefore whoever resists the authority resists the ordinance of God, and those who resist will bring judgment on themselves. For rulers are not a terror to good works, but to evil... For he is* <u>*God's minister*</u> *to you for good. But if you do evil, be afraid; for he does not bear the sword in vain; for he is* <u>*God's minister*</u>*, an avenger to execute wrath on him who practices evil. (Romans 13:1–4 emphasis added)*

God Himself established government as a social institution. Therefore, everyone is under an authority and must submit to it. You will remember in message five that laws, and the government that enforces them, are for our protection and peace. Therefore, those who resist that authority are actually resisting the Lord and will be condemned. Why? The passage above makes it clear: rulers are God's ministers or servants. He ordains them specifically to restrain evil and promote good—your good!

What about bad rulers and abusive authorities? It is true that not everyone does their job properly or takes their responsibility seriously. The Lord, as

King over all, has provisions for these cases also. When He said, "every soul," He means everyone.

> *The God of Israel said,*
>   *The Rock of Israel spoke to me:*
>   *"He who rules over men must be just,*
>   *Ruling in the fear of God." (2 Samuel 23:3)*

Rulers are subject to God's laws also. If they break His laws, they are to be held accountable. For this reason, the Apostle Paul said,

> *Therefore I exhort first of all that supplications, prayers, interces-sions, and giving of thanks be made for all men, for kings and all who are in authority, that we may lead a quiet and peaceable life in all godliness and reverence. (1 Timothy 2:1–2)*

We are to pray for government, leaders, and authorities that they would make good and right decisions to promote the welfare of all people. If they pervert justice instead, remember that their authority is limited.

> *Peter and the other apostles answered and said: "We ought to obey God rather than men." (Acts 5:29b)*

No matter what an authority says, we must obey the Lord. He is the King of the universe, and His laws are supreme over the planet. That is why we all share the duty to speak out against evil, as God had His prophets do in ancient times. For example, Daniel told King Nebuchadnezzar,

> *"Therefore, O king, let my advice be acceptable to you; break off your sins by being righteous, and your iniquities by showing mercy to the poor." (Daniel 4:27a)*

Authorities doing what is right is so important to the Almighty that He gave them explicit instructions to rule justly. For another example, consider when He spoke through the psalmist:

> *Now therefore, be wise, O kings;*
> *Be instructed, you judges of the earth.*
> *Serve the LORD with fear,*
> *And rejoice with trembling. (Psalm 2:10–11)*

Rulers are to be wise and carry out their duties with the fear of God in their hearts. Why? Because the sovereign One is coming back to Earth.

A Physical Kingdom Is Coming

> *Keep this commandment without spot, blameless until our Lord Jesus Christ's appearing...He who is the blessed and only Potentate, the King of kings and Lord of lords. (1 Timothy 6:14–15)*

Jesus is the King of kings and Lord of lords. One day He is coming back to visibly rule this world.

> *For unto us a Child is born,*
> *Unto us a Son is given;*
> *And the government will be upon His shoulder.*
> *And His name will be called*
> *Wonderful, Counselor, Mighty God,*
> *Everlasting Father, Prince of Peace.*
> *Of the increase of His government and peace*
> *There will be no end,*
> *Upon the throne of David and over His kingdom,*
> *To order it and establish it with judgment and justice*
> *From that time forward, even forever.*
> *The zeal of the LORD of hosts will perform this. (Isaiah 9:6–7)*

The Mighty God will have justice forever in His kingdom. The Prince of Peace will bring peace to His people. Yet He warns,

> *"There is no peace," says the LORD, "for the wicked." (Isaiah 48:22)*

The wicked cannot have peace. Even if their lives seem good on the outside, they are in turmoil within. Even worse, they cannot have peace with God because they actively fight against Him.

How about you? Is there peace between you and God? As King, He will welcome you into His kingdom if you surrender the fight against His authority.

> *And Jesus came and spoke to them, saying, "All authority has been given to Me in heaven and on earth." (Matthew 28:18)*

Jesus has all authority. He rules the universe, yet He lets us choose if He can reign in our hearts. One day everyone *will* submit to His authority. Today Jesus *invites* us to submit and be saved.

> *Look to Me, and be saved,*
>   *All you ends of the earth!*
>   *For I am God, and there is no other.*
>   *I have sworn by Myself;*
>   *The word has gone out of My mouth in righteousness,*
>   *And shall not return,*
>   *That to Me every knee shall bow,*
>   *Every tongue shall take an oath...*
>   *And all shall be ashamed*
>   *Who are incensed against Him. (Isaiah 45:22–24)*

Our Creator reminds us that He is the only God and He alone can save. As Sovereign, He has decreed every knee will bow to Him. Those who bow in surrender to Jesus now will be saved and blessed. Those who wait will be condemned.

Have you chosen to submit to God's authority? Are you willing to have Jesus as your king? Let Him be the king that not only rules, but loves and protects your soul, just as we saw the shepherd do for the sheep.

Think About It

1. God is king over the universe, but what does it mean for Him to be your king?

2. What is the relationship between the Lord and earthly authorities?

3. How easy or hard is it for you to submit to God as your king? Does it make a difference knowing that He cares for His subjects like a shepherd cares for his sheep?

Message 15 – I Am Judge

Let's continue to ask, who is God? The Lord has given several messages from Heaven about who He is so that we can better know Him.

> **For the LORD is our Judge,**
> **The LORD is our Lawgiver,**
> **The LORD is our King;**
> **He will save us. (Isaiah 33:22)**

This is an insightful description of three of the Almighty's roles and responsibilities. It is also where society first learned the idea of a balance of power in a divided government.

With humans, the saying "absolute power corrupts absolutely" is true because of our sinful nature. History has demonstrated this time after time. Therefore, people came to realize that power should be divided or shared, and a system of checks and balances was born in the age of modern government. For example, we have judges who interpret laws, legislators who create laws, and executives (the function of the king) who enforce laws. Isn't it amazing? God expressed this concept thousands of years ago, but it was only a few hundred years ago that people decided to take His advice!

Going back to who God is, why doesn't absolute power cause problems for Him? The answer is simple—God has no sin. Therefore, He is not selfish and always uses power properly. Of course, we have limited knowledge and cannot see all the facts all the time, so it may appear to us that the Lord has been unfair at times. Yet, like a parent who sees the big picture that eludes the children who are only focused on the toy or candy in front of them, the Lord acts according to His wisdom instead of our immediate wants.

Breaking down Isaiah 33:22, we see God is our Judge, Lawgiver, and King. We just talked about Him being our King in the previous message. In "Rules Are Good for You" we saw Him as the Lawgiver. So, what does it mean that God is our Judge, as the start of the verse tells us, and that He will save us, as the end of the verse promises?

A judge hears cases, complaints, and causes. He weighs the evidence and decides who is guilty or innocent. He declares who is right or wrong, pronounces sentences, and imposes fines or punishment. All this is done in pursuit of justice.

God Wants Justice

The Bible frequently talks about God wanting and requiring justice. For example,

> *God stands in the congregation of the mighty;*
> *He judges among the gods [or mighty ones].*
> *How long will you judge unjustly,*
> *And show partiality to the wicked?*
> *Defend the poor and fatherless;*
> *Do justice to the afflicted and needy. (Psalm 82:1–3)*

This reinforces what we saw in message four, that God gave government to restrain evil. His desire is for us to

> *Learn to do good;*
> *Seek justice,*

Rebuke the oppressor;
Defend the fatherless,
Plead for the widow. (Isaiah 1:17)

These principles of doing right, bringing justice to the oppressed, and protecting vulnerable people from exploitation echo throughout the Bible.

God is the Judge of all the Earth (Genesis 18:25). Therefore, He will bring justice.

> **But we know that the judgment of God is according to truth. (Romans 2:2a)**

Since He is God, we can be sure He will judge based on truth. This isn't just an inference we can make from His nature, but a promise He has made:

> *For He is coming, for He is coming to judge the earth.*
> *He shall judge the world with righteousness,*
> *And the peoples with His truth. (Psalm 96:13)*

The Lord judges in righteousness and truth, and He will judge everyone on the planet. We saw that in message one when Jesus told us He will separate the good from the bad as a shepherd separates sheep from goats (Matthew 25:31–40). For those who rebel, there is coming

> **the day of wrath and revelation of the righteous judgment of God, who "will render to each one according to his deeds." (Romans 2:5b–6)**

In message ten, we saw that people want to be judged by their deeds in a false hope that their good will outweigh the bad. The truth is that our deeds will condemn us. As Vernon McGee wrote, "He shall reward every man according to his works. Absolute justice is the criterion of judgment or reward. Man's deeds stand before God in His holy light. No man in his right mind wants to be judged on this basis."[7] Why not? No person's deeds are good enough to deserve Heaven. Yet, those who trust in themselves will get their chance at the last judgment.

> *Then I saw a great white throne and Him who sat on it, from whose face the earth and the heaven fled away...And I saw the dead, small and great, standing before God, and books were opened...And the dead were judged according to their works, by the things which were written in the books. (Revelation 20:11-12)*

One day every soul will give an account to God. Those who have accepted Jesus escape the final judgment (John 3:16). Those who do not will stand before the great white throne where God, the great Judge of the universe, will dispense final justice. Rich and poor, famous and unknown, rulers and subjects—all will be judged by their works. Jesus testified that the Lord has accurately recorded everyone's deeds in the books of Heaven:

> *"For there is nothing covered that will not be revealed, nor hidden that will not be known. Therefore whatever you have spoken in the dark will be heard in the light, and what you have spoken in the ear in inner rooms will be proclaimed on the housetops." (Luke 12:2-3)*

The Lord sees all and knows all. This is why He can judge 100 percent righteously. If this is scary, and it should be, think of how kind God is to warn us many times in the Bible so that we can be prepared.[8]

> *For God will bring every work into judgment,*

---

[7] *Thru the Bible with J. Vernon McGee*, Vol 4, pp 657-658, J. Vernon McGee, Thomas Nelson Publishers, 1983.

[8] Psalm 62:12, Jeremiah 17:10, Matthew 16:17, 2 Corinthians 5:10

Including every secret thing,
Whether good or evil. (Ecclesiastes 12:14)

If we take heed to the warnings, we have no need to fear the judgment. Those who trust Jesus as Savior will have their names written in a special book in Heaven, the Book of Life.

The Book of Life

And I urge you also, true companion, help these women who labored with me in the gospel, with Clement also, and the rest of my fellow workers, whose names are in the Book of Life. (Philippians 4:3)

The famous Apostle Paul was discussing those who had helped him serve Jesus and said their names were written in the Book of Life. Moses and God talked about this book in Exodus 32: 31–33. Jesus mentioned this idea to His disciples in Luke 10:20. Therefore, we get complete assurance of safety on judgment day. On the other hand,

anyone <u>not</u> found written in the Book of Life was cast into the lake of fire. (Revelation 20:15 emphasis added)

Those whose names are not written in the Book of Life are sentenced to eternal fire at the judgment because they trusted in themselves and their works instead of trusting in Jesus. Those who trust in Jesus are safe with a home in Heaven.

"For God did not send His Son into the world to condemn the world, but that the world through Him might be saved.
He who believes in Him is not condemned; but he who does not believe is condemned already, because he has not believed in the name of the only begotten Son of God." (John 3:17–18)

God sent Jesus to Earth the first time to save us. When He comes the second time, it will be to judge the world. Those who don't believe will suffer the verdict of condemnation for their sinful deeds. If you have not believed, I urge you, trust the Lord today so that you can escape the final judgment! If you have believed, are you helping others escape the judgment?

Think About It

1. Why is it good that God has absolute power to make laws and enforce them? (Hint: What does God not have?)

2. Will the Lord judge every person? How do we know?

3. How can you escape condemnation at the final judgment?

Message 16 – I Am Love

People like the idea of a kind and loving God. The Lord is kind and loving as we have seen, so what does He say about His love? Is it the type of love we think of, or is it something else? Let's get some quick background on what the Almighty says about human love to set the stage for a fascinating discussion.

We encounter the first mention of man loving God when the Lord gave the Ten Commandments. When discussing punishment for the guilty, God said He shows

> *"mercy to thousands, to those who love Me and keep My commandments." (Exodus 20:6)*

God promised mercy to those who love and obey. In this verse, the word for love in the original language means "to have affection for."[9] Thus, there is a blessing for those who really like God—for those who are attached to or are fond of Him. This is the same word God uses in the command to care for others.

> *"You shall not take vengeance, nor bear any grudge against the children of your people, but you shall love your neighbor as yourself: I am the LORD." (Leviticus 19:18)*

---

[9] *Strong's* Hebrew definition number 157.

We are to care for others just as we care for ourselves.

How Does God Love?

The first mention of God's love for people uses the same word to show affection.

> *"And because He loved your fathers, therefore He chose their descendants after them; and He brought you out of Egypt with His Presence, with His mighty power." (Deuteronomy 4:37)*

Yet God loves us in a different way as well.

> *"The LORD did not set His love on you nor choose you because you were more in number than any other people, for you were the least of all peoples." (Deuteronomy 7:7)*

Moses told the Israelites that God set (put or placed) His love upon them; that is, He chose to love them. This is important for us to see: love is a choice, not just a feeling. What kind of love is God talking about putting on people? The word for love in this verse means "to cling, i.e. join, (figuratively) to love, delight in."[10]

The Lord actively chooses to love humans, to cling to us and delight in us. It is also critical to notice that God doesn't choose anyone because of their status or what they have to offer. God loves because He chose to give His love, not because we earned it.

When you read through the Bible, you will notice that we humans are told to love the Lord many times. For example, Deuteronomy 6:5, Joshua 22:5, Psalm 31:23, Matthew 22:37, John 14:15, etc. The Lord talks about His love

---

[10] *Strong's* Hebrew definition number 2836.

for us, but not as frequently. Why? God's love is steadfast.

> *The LORD has appeared of old to me, saying:*
> *"Yes, I have loved you with an everlasting love;*
> *Therefore with lovingkindness I have drawn you." (Jeremiah*
> *31:3)*

God's love does not fade like ours. We need the reminders, not Him. What else does God say about Himself and love?

> *God is love, and he who abides in love abides in God, and God in*
> *him. (1 John 4:16b)*

God is love! What does that mean? Is He a feeling or emotion? No, the Greek word translated as love in this verse is *agape*. It means "to have esteem" or "high regard."[11] "It is primarily a love of the will."[12] You may think of it in these terms: I esteem (love) you so much, I'm going to put your interests ahead of my own. This love or high esteem is a choice, as we saw earlier. It does not need an emotion. It is not dependent upon the person being loved or their actions or how good they are. This is real love, and the Bible declares, "God is the personification of perfect love."[13]

God's perfect love is sacrificial.

> *"For God so loved the world that He gave His only begotten Son, that*
> *whoever believes in Him should not perish but have everlasting*
> *life." (John 3:16)*

The Lord gave His Son to pay for our sin and rescue us. This is the greatest

---

[11] Youngblood, p. 775 "Love."

[12] Youngblood, p. 27 "Agape."

[13] Youngblood, p. 775 "Love."

love in the universe. In fact, Jesus said,

> *"Greater love has no one than this, than to lay down one's life for his friends." (John 15:13)*

Jesus willingly laid down His life to save us and make us His friends. He both demonstrated and proved God's great love for us. This love is available to all.

> *For "whoever calls on the name of the Lord shall be saved."* *(Romans 10:13 emphasis added)*

Whoever includes you! Yet the good news gets better. Once you have accepted God's love, He will not take it away.

Permanent Love

> *Who shall separate us from the love of Christ?*
> *For I am persuaded that neither death nor life, nor angels nor principalities nor powers, nor things present nor things to come, nor height nor depth, nor any other created thing, shall be able to separate us from the love of God which is in Christ Jesus our Lord. (Romans 8:35a, 38–39)*

Nothing can separate God's children from His love. This is a powerful truth. Once we are in God's family, we have eternal security. This is because our Lord is so powerful, not because of our own merit or strength. He saves and keeps us saved. Our response is to love Him back.

> *We love Him because He first loved us. (1 John 4:19)*

God loved first and we respond. How do we show love for God? Jesus said,

> *"If you love Me, keep My commandments." (John 14:15)*

At times you will likely have the warm emotional feeling of love toward God. But remember, feelings come and go; real love does not. Show real love toward God by being steadfast in living for Him, even when you don't feel like it. How do you love when you don't feel like it? Remember why you love (because He loves you), then choose to do it. As we said before, love is a choice.

We obey out of love, gratitude, reverence, and affection for the One who gave all for us. This is why all the rules in all the world could be summarized or better stated as two simple commandments.

> *Jesus said to him, "You shall love the Lord your God with all your heart, with all your soul, and with all your mind.' This is the first and great commandment. And the second is like it: 'You shall love your neighbor as yourself.' On these two commandments hang all the Law and the Prophets." (Matthew 22:37–40)*

Now is the time to receive God's love and love Him in return. This will allow a person to love others properly, to look out for their wellbeing, to treat them fairly, and to help when needed. In doing so, we will be sharing the love of God. Everyone needs His love, and those who accept it are blessed. Try sharing God's love today and watch your love increase.

Think About It

1. Have you ever thought about real love being both a choice and sacrifice? How is this different from our culture's concept of love?

2. What is the greatest act of love? And who did it? (Hint: John 15:13)

3. Why can all rules and laws be summarized with only two commands to love? How would our lives and world be different if we faithfully loved God and loved others?

Message 17 – I Am Holy

Of all the words we associate with God, which do you think describes Him best? Which do you think God most associates with Himself? A good argument can be made for the word holy. On two occasions, both scenes of heavenly glory, the word appears in eye-catching fashion.

> *And one [angelic being] cried to another and said:*
> *"Holy, holy, holy is the LORD of hosts;*
> *The whole earth is full of His glory!" (Isaiah 6:3)*

> *The four living creatures, each having six wings, were full of eyes around and within. And they do not rest day or night, saying:*
> *"Holy, holy, holy,*
> *Lord God Almighty,*
> *Who was and is and is to come!" (Revelation 4:8)*

The Bible never says that God is "love, love, love" or "just, just, just." Yet, in both the Old and New Testament, heavenly beings declare our Lord is "holy, holy, holy." Obviously, this repetition is used to emphasize how important the Almighty considers the trait to be. So, what does this important word mean?

What Does Holy Actually Mean?

When the term holy appears in the Old Testament, it most often is translated from a Hebrew word meaning "to be (ceremonially or morally) clean or to make, pronounce or observe as clean."[14] It often refers to "a sacred place or thing."[15] We see this the very first time holy is used in the Bible, when God talked with Moses from the burning bush.

> *Then He said, "Do not draw near this place. Take your sandals off your feet, for the place where you stand is holy ground." (Exodus 3:5)*

The place where the Lord met Moses was holy or sacred. In other instances, we see the word holy applied to people. Here God uses the word in that context for the first time:

> *"For I am the LORD your God. You shall therefore consecrate yourselves, and you shall be holy; for I am holy. Neither shall you defile yourselves... You shall therefore be holy, for I am holy." (Leviticus 11:44–45)*

God told His people to "consecrate" themselves. Consecrate comes from the same Hebrew word for holy that means to make clean. They were to be sacred, or morally and ceremonially clean, because that is how He is! How is God "clean"?

> *"He is the Rock, His work is perfect;*
>   *For all His ways are justice,*
>   *A God of truth and without injustice;*
>   *Righteous and upright is He." (Deuteronomy 32:4)*

God's work and ways are perfectly right. He is a God of truth. He is just and righteous. He is without iniquity. That means no evil, no dirt, no corruption.

---

[14] *Strong's* Hebrew definition number 6942.

[15] *Strong's* Hebrew definition number 6944.

God is perfectly clean from sin. (This truth is repeated in Psalm 119:137.)

We saw previously that God cannot stand sin. Therefore, in order for Him to fellowship with us, we must be clean. For example, He said,

> *"Wash yourselves, make yourselves clean;*
>   *Put away the evil of your doings from before My eyes.*
>   *Cease to do evil." (Isaiah 1:16)*

We must be cleansed from sin in order for the Lord to look favorably on us. In fact, we must be clean to approach a holy God. The Lord illustrated this requirement with the sacrificial system of the Old Testament.

> *"Thus Aaron shall come into the Holy Place: with the blood of a young bull as a sin offering, and of a ram as a burnt offering. He shall put the holy linen tunic and the linen trousers on his body; he shall be girded with a linen sash, and with the linen turban he shall be attired. These are holy garments. Therefore he shall wash his body in water, and put them on." (Leviticus 16:3–4)*

Before the high priest could go into the holy place with an offering, he had to wash and put on holy garments. Once the priest was ceremonially clean, he could bring the sacrifice for sin to address moral cleansing (Leviticus 16:5–16). Remember, this is why the Lord sent Jesus as the ultimate and final sacrifice for sin (Hebrews 10:10–12).

Therefore, it should not be a surprise that the New Testament word for holy most often comes from a term meaning "sacred (physically pure, morally blameless or religious, ceremonially consecrated)."[16] The idea is someone or something set apart from normal use for a sacred purpose. Jesus rescued us from sin that we might be special for Him:

---

[16] *Strong's* Greek definition number 40.

*Husbands, love your wives, just as Christ also loved the church and gave Himself for her, that **He might sanctify and cleanse her** with the washing of water by the word. (Ephesians 5:25b–26 emphasis added)*

Jesus' sacrifice made the way for sinners to be clean and have access to our loving yet holy God. What should our response be?

Therefore, having these promises, beloved, let us cleanse ourselves from all filthiness of the flesh and spirit, perfecting holiness in the fear of God. (2 Corinthians 7:1)

Since God has done so much for us and given salvation through Jesus, we should live clean lives for Him. How? By purifying ourselves or removing that which defiles or corrupts our mind and spirit. That means we turn away from, let go of, and get rid of sinful habits, thought patterns, and language. This is practically impossible for us humans, which is why the Lord does not leave us to live holy on our own. When Jesus told His followers to obey, He promised to help them obey.

Holy Help

"If you love Me, keep My commandments. And I will pray the Father, and He will give you another Helper, that He may abide with you forever—the Spirit of truth, whom the world cannot receive, because it neither sees Him nor knows Him; but you know Him, for He dwells with you and will be in you." (John 14:15–17a)

The "Helper" is the Holy Spirit—God living in us, leading and empowering us to live holy lives. This is great news! We don't have to be holy on our own. For example,

This is the word of the LORD to Zerubbabel:

81

"Not by might nor by power, but by My Spirit,"
Says the LORD of hosts. (Zechariah 4:6)

When God gave Zerubbabel a very hard task, He said it would not be accomplished with human power. Dr. McGee put it this way: "It's not by brawn nor by brain, but by My Spirit. It will not be by your cleverness, your ability, or your physical strength."[17] It would be done through the Holy Spirit. Again, the Lord said,

"I will put My Spirit within you and cause you to walk in My statutes, and you will keep My judgments and do them." (Ezekiel 36:27)

The Holy Spirit enables us to live holy because He lives in us. We must choose whether to obey or not, but He gives us the ability. Consider this:

Or do you not know that your body is the temple of the Holy Spirit who is in you, whom you have from God, and you are not your own? For you were bought at a price; therefore glorify God in your body and in your spirit, which are God's. (1 Corinthians 6:19–20)

We belong to our Creator, so we should bring Him glory with our body and spirit. We do this by providing a welcoming home, a clean home, for His Holy Spirit. You can begin to do this by thinking clean thoughts.

Finally, brethren, whatever things are true, whatever things are noble, whatever things are just, whatever things are pure, whatever things are lovely, whatever things are of good report, if there is any virtue and if there is anything praiseworthy— meditate on these things. (Philippians 4:8)

---

[17] McGee, Vol. 3, p. 923.

Then meditate on God's word and obey it.

> *How can a young man [or woman] cleanse his way?*
> *By taking heed according to Your word. (Psalm 119:9)*

Think About It

1. What does holy mean, and why is it a good description for God?

2. Why does the Lord want us to be holy?

3. Can we be holy on our own? Who did God send to make and keep us holy?

Message 18 – I Am Powerful

The most obvious characteristic of God is His power as, by definition, a deity must have supernatural power. Then why does the Lord take time to tell us of His power and abilities? There is a direct relationship between our understanding of God's power and how we live. So, what does He say about power? Recall this passage from message 11:

> **God has spoken once,**
> **Twice I have heard this:**
> **That power belongs to God. (Psalm 62:11)**

The Lord said power belongs to Him. He is the source of strength, authority, and ability. For example, God has the power to create.

> **All things were made through Him, and without Him nothing was made that was made. (John 1:3)**

It takes great power to create a universe, so the Creation testifies of God's power.

> **The heavens declare the glory of God;**
> **And the firmament [or sky] shows His handiwork. (Psalm 19:1)**

Just in case you thought the universe made itself, the Lord reminds us,

84

Thus says the LORD:
"Heaven is My throne,
And earth is My footstool...
For all those things My hand has made,
And all those things exist,"
Says the LORD. (Isaiah 66:1a, 2a)

Who Is in Charge?

The Lord not only made the universe, He controls it.

O LORD God of hosts,
Who is mighty like You, O LORD?...
You rule the raging of the sea;
When its waves rise, You still them...
You have a mighty arm;
Strong is Your hand, and high is Your right hand. (Psalm 89:8a,
9, 13)

Ruling the sea is one example of the Creator's power over nature and shows how strong He is.

God also has power over nations (Psalm 2) and rulers. The Bible states,

The Most High rules in the kingdom of men,
Gives it to whomever He will,
And sets over it the lowest of men. (Daniel 4:17b)

He demonstrates His divine power by deciding who can lead, when, and where. Consider when God had Moses confront Pharaoh, king of Egypt.

"Thus says the LORD God of the Hebrews: 'Let My people go, that
they may serve Me, for at this time I will send all My plagues to

your very heart, and on your servants and on your people, that
you may know that there is none like Me in all the earth... But
indeed for this purpose I have raised you up, that I may show My
power in you, and that My name may be declared in all the earth.'"
(Exodus 9:13b–14, 16)

Pharaoh thought he was in charge and in control. But the Lord let us know that He only put Pharaoh on the throne so that God's name would be declared around the world. The king's stubborn attempt to keep Israel enslaved gave God cause to bring the ten plagues upon Egypt and reveal His incredible power. Humans have never seen anything like it before or since, and these proved the Lord alone is the Almighty.

The Lord has also showed power over disease. For example, He healed king Hezekiah of a deadly disease (2 Kings 20). He healed Naaman of leprosy and caused him to say,

> *"Indeed, now I know that there is no God in all the earth, except in*
> *Israel." (2 Kings 5:15b)*

You've probably heard stories of the multitudes of people Jesus healed, demonstrating divine power. Here is an example.

> *When evening had come, they brought to Him many who were*
> *demon-possessed. And He cast out the spirits with a word, and*
> *healed all who were sick, that it might be fulfilled which was spoken*
> *by Isaiah the prophet, saying:*
> *"He Himself took our infirmities*
> *And bore our sicknesses." (Matthew 8:16–17)*

Not only can God heal disease, He has power over evil spirits (Matthew 8:28–34). Thus, we see God has power over things natural and unnatural, over things spiritual and physical.

The Bible records many examples of the Lord's power so that we can know He is the Almighty. What does this mean for us? Since He is the Creator, we belong to Him. Since He is the greatest, we must listen when He speaks. Since He is the King of kings, we must obey His laws. Since He is the Almighty, He has the power to do what He says, so we can trust him! Therefore, when Jesus says He can forgive sins and take you to Heaven, we can believe it!

Ultimate Power

As if all the evidence we've seen was not enough, Jesus demonstrated power over life and death to provide certainty of His ability to give eternal life.

> *And the LORD God formed man of the dust of the ground, and breathed into his nostrils the breath of life; and man became a living being. (Genesis 2:7)*

God is the author of life. He made all living creatures in the beginning. Then He made man special. He breathed into the first human the breath of life. He gave man a soul.

The Lord has power over death as seen when the prophet Elisha raised a boy to life (2 Kings 4:32-26). We also see this in Ezekiel's famous experience in the valley of dry bones.

> *"Therefore prophesy and say to them, Thus says the LORD God: "Behold, O My people, I will open your graves and cause you to come up from your graves, and bring you into the land of Israel. Then you shall know that I am the LORD, when I have opened your graves."" (Ezekiel 37:12–13a)*

Why did God promise to bring people back from death? So that they would know He is the Lord God.

Of course, Jesus raised the dead during His earthly ministry. He raised the widow's son (Luke 7:12–16), Jairus's daughter (Mark 5:35–42), and Lazarus (John 11:1–46).

Power to raise the dead is unimaginable, yet even greater than that is power to bring oneself back from the dead. Jesus said,

> *"Therefore My Father loves Me, because I lay down My life that I may take it again. No one takes it from Me, but I lay it down of Myself. I have power to lay it down, and I have power to take it again." (John 10:17–18a)*

Jesus has complete authority over His life. He chose to die for us, and He chose to come back from the dead. After He rose from the dead,

> *Jesus came and spoke to them, saying, "All authority has been given to Me in heaven and on earth. Go therefore and make disciples of all the nations." (Matthew 28:18–19a)*

Jesus proved it and declared it: He has all power over all the universe. He is God! Therefore, we are to believe, obey, and tell others about Him. This is why we have the Bible.

> *And truly Jesus did many other signs in the presence of His disciples, which are not written in this book; but these are written that you may believe that Jesus is the Christ, the Son of God, and that believing you may have life in His name. (John 20:30–31)*

Our faith is not in myths and legends. We don't serve a little deity contrived by human imagination. Our faith is in a risen Savior who proved and documented His power so we can believe and go to Heaven!

Think About It

1. God has power over nature, people, and spirits. This covers things both physical and _____. Is there anything left out?

2. Since God has all power, what should our response be when He speaks?

3. Jesus demonstrated power over life and death. How does this prove His ability to save your soul and take you to Heaven?

Message 19 – I Am the Only God

Is there more than one God? There are many religions, but do they have the same deity? For example, ancient Egypt and Rome were known for having multiple gods. Even today, Hinduism claims multiple deities. The Bible explains that humanity once knew the one true God but turned away to their own inventions:

> *Because, although they knew God, they did not glorify Him as God, nor were thankful, but became futile in their thoughts, and their foolish hearts were darkened. Professing to be wise, they became fools, and changed the glory of the incorruptible God into an image made like corruptible man—and birds and four-footed animals and creeping things. (Romans 1:21–23)*

Religion Is Against God

Throughout recorded history, people have not been thankful to their Creator. Though He had blessed us with life and given a world of food and resources, we were not satisfied. We wanted more and we wanted to be in charge. Instead of gratitude toward God, our thinking vainly focused on ourselves. In pride we thought we were as smart as God. So, we remade Him into something of our own likeness, something we could understand, something we could control. Whether it was an actual thing like an idol, an invisible force like nature, or something of desire like power, pleasure, or money, people invented systems of worship so they could control the deity. The objective of religion is to please the deity with actions, offerings, or prayers—so that the deity will then give you what you want.

All non-biblical religious beliefs share the same origin, whether they are part of an established religion or simply what feels like truth to a given individual. In pride with vain thinking, humans exchanged the true divine glory for something of their own invention. Thus, all religions have the same deity, a **Not-God**. We can be 100 percent sure that people who do not follow Jesus are not worshiping God, based on this testimony from the Almighty:

> *"You are My witnesses," says the LORD,*
>   *"And My servant whom I have chosen,*
>   *That you may know and believe Me,*
>   *And understand that I am He.*
>   *Before Me there was no God formed,*
>   *Nor shall there be after Me.*
>   *I, even I, am the LORD,*
>   *And besides Me there is no savior." (Isaiah 43:10–11)*

The Lord demonstrated His power to prove He is the self-existing One. There was no God before Him. There is not another God coming. He is the Lord and the only Savior. Just in case you were not sure, He said it again:

> *Thus says the LORD, the King of Israel,*
>   *And his Redeemer, the LORD of hosts:*
>   *"I am the First and I am the Last;*
>   *Besides Me there is no God." (Isaiah 44:6)*

The Lord is the eternal One, the First and Last. He is the only God. He told us this many times to dispel the foolish notion that anyone other than Him was or ever could be in charge.[18] For example,

> *We know that an idol is nothing in the world, and that there is no other God but one. (1 Corinthians 8:4b)*

Why Is This Important?

Why is this such a big deal? Why does it matter if we think there is another deity or not?

> *"I am the LORD, that is My name;*
> *And My glory I will not give to another,*
> *Nor My praise to carved images." (Isaiah 42:8)*

The Lord will not share His glory with anyone, and He should not. There are at least two reasons for this.

First, as the Almighty, God deserves His glory. To give His glory to anyone else is a terrible offense against the Lord. The Bible recounts how King Herod gave a speech and his audience said it was the voice of a god and not a man. Herod accepted the glory, which was an egregious insult to the Lord, so God struck him dead (Acts 12:21–24).

The second reason the Lord should not share His glory with anyone is that it would be very bad for us. If we thought anyone or anything was on the same level with the Almighty, we might look to the other deity for guidance, protection, provision, or most importantly salvation. The end result is that we would end up in Hell because we did not accept Jesus as the only God who can save us (Acts 4:12). Please don't miss this critical truth.

---

[18] Exodus 8:10, Deuteronomy 33:26, 2 Samuel 7:22, 1 Kings 8:23, 1 Chronicles 17:20, Psalm 83:8, Psalm 86:10, Isaiah 45:18 and 22, Ephesians 4:6, etc.

For there is one God and one Mediator between God and men, the Man Christ Jesus. (1 Timothy 2:5)

One God. One Savior. Jesus is our only hope.

At this point you might wonder how Jesus could be God, if there truly is only one God. Jesus explained by saying,

"I and My Father are one." (John 10:30)

Jesus declared He was one with the Lord God the Father. He also provided evidence in the form of miracles when He walked on Earth. Jesus said,

"If I do not do the works of My Father, do not believe Me; but if I do, though you do not believe Me, believe the works, that you may know and believe that the Father is in Me, and I in Him." (John 10: 37–38)

The amazing power Jesus demonstrated, which we discussed in the previous message, is evidence that He told the truth. What about the Holy Spirit?

For there are three that bear witness in heaven: the Father, the Word, and the Holy Spirit; and these three are one. (1 John 5:7)

God tells us He is one God in three persons. God the Father, God the Son (Jesus, called the Word), and God the Holy Spirit are one Being. This is a supernatural concept, so it is difficult for natural minds to comprehend. (It may help to think in terms of multiplication rather than addition. God could be $1 \times 1 \times 1 = 1$. He would not be $1 + 1 + 1 = 3$.) Whatever we think about the concept, God said it, so we can believe it. This is why God told Moses to say,

"Hear, O Israel: The LORD our God, the LORD is one! You shall love the LORD your God with all your heart, with all your soul,

and with all your strength." (Deuteronomy 6:4–5)

In these verses, the Hebrew word for LORD is singular but the word for God is plural.[19] Our Creator went out of His way to tell us He is One so that we would love Him. We are to love Him with all our being—that is, with all our might. Our love is not to be divided between the Lord and anyone else. In fact, Jesus told us it is impossible to really love two masters or two supernatural authorities (Matthew 6:24). Now are you starting to understand why it is important to know there is one God? Moses gave us a nice summary of the reason.

> *"Therefore know this day, and consider it in your heart, that the LORD Himself is God in heaven above and on the earth beneath; there is no other. You shall therefore keep His statutes and His commandments which I command you today, that it may go well with you and with your children after you, and that you may prolong your days in the land which the LORD your God is giving you for all time." (Deuteronomy 4:39–40)*

Think About It

1. Why did humans invent religions with deities who are not God?

2. What are two reasons God does not and should not share His glory with anyone or anything?

3. Why is it important for us to know there is only one God?

---

[19] *Strong's* Hebrew definition number 430.

Message 20 – You Are Not God

Since there is only one God, why do some religions say that we can become gods? And why do some people live like they are their own gods?

Remember how Satan tempted Adam and Eve with the idea that "you will be like God" (Genesis 3:5)? Why was this even a temptation? People like being their own bosses. We want to live how we choose. We want to make the rules. We want things our way.

If you want evidence of these statements, ask yourself, "Do I like being told what to do?" The answer is No! You allow some people and some authorities to tell you what to do because you don't want the consequences of noncompliance.

As a society, we realized civilization would fall apart if everyone made their own rules, as we discussed in message five. Yet, when we hear that we can be a god, it gives the false hope that one day we can make life's rules, or at least escape them. This is why people are drawn to religions that promise they can achieve deity status themselves. (It is also why atheists deny God exists, so they can take His place and live as they please.)

Even for religions that don't allow you to become a deity, they claim that by following certain rules, you can make their deity do what you want. They promote silly doctrines such as "if you do A+B+C, then the deity must do X+Y+Z for you." Even corrupted versions of Christianity claim that the Lord is obligated to give what you want if you do what the preacher says. All of these lies are just another way of getting you in a position to control God, which means you are in charge.

Satan, whose original name was Lucifer, was once a powerful and beautiful angel. In pride he tried to overthrow the Lord who had made him. What happened?

> *How you are fallen from heaven,*
> *O Lucifer, son of the morning!*
> *How you are cut down to the ground,*
> *You who weakened the nations!*
> *For you have said in your heart:*
> *"I will ascend into heaven,*
> *I will exalt my throne above the stars of God;*
> *I will also sit on the mount of the congregation*
> *On the farthest sides of the north;*
> *I will ascend above the heights of the clouds,*
> *I will be like the Most High." (Isaiah 14:12–14)*

Lucifer was proud and said in his heart, "I will," five times. Here was the "son of the morning" who tried to be God. He was cast down and humiliated; God pronounced judgment on him, and Lucifer has an eternal lake of fire waiting for him (Revelation 20:10). If an angel cannot be God, why do we think we can? The answer is pride. Thankfully, our Creator gives us help to know our limitations.

You Are Limited, God Is Not

> *"Which of you by worrying can add one cubit to his stature?"*
> *(Matthew 6:27)*

In this rhetorical question, Jesus pointed out that we humans lack the ability to increase our height by our own cleverness or problem-solving abilities. In fact, not only are we limited, but we are beset by weaknesses within and without.

> *"Watch and pray, lest you enter into temptation. The spirit indeed is willing, but the flesh is weak." (Matthew 26:41)*

Jesus warned that even if inside we want to do good, our flesh is weak, so we must be on guard and pray. Thus, the weakness of our bodies, our physical limitations, should remind us that we are not God. Pastor David Platt put it this way, "The reason you get tired and need sleep is because you are not God. While you sleep at night, the Lord keeps the world going. Your abilities, intelligence, and plans all have to stop at night and rely on God."[20]

Think for a minute. What would happen if you or any other human were God? You wouldn't be strong enough to maintain the laws of nature, and things would fly apart. Or the fickle human mind would cause the rules to change so much that the world would fall into chaos.

In the book of Job, the Bible records a mighty debate. Job and his brainy friends argued about the great issues and questions of life. Finally, the Lord joined in to remind them—and us—we are not God.

> *Then the LORD answered Job out of the whirlwind, and said:*
> *"Who is this who darkens counsel*
> *By words without knowledge?*
> *Now prepare yourself like a man;*
> *I will question you, and you shall answer Me.*
> *"Where were you when I laid the foundations of the earth?*
> *Tell Me, if you have understanding." (Job 38:1–4)*

---

[20] David Platt sermon "You Are Not God", McLean Bible Church, Vienna, Virginia 2021.

Human words and wisdom won't get you far in a discussion with the Almighty. He can ask questions you cannot answer. For example, "Where were you when I made the world?" Oh, you did not yet exist.

> *"Or who shut in the sea with doors,*
> *When it burst forth and issued from the womb?" (Job 38:8)*

Who gave the mighty oceans a boundary? Not you.

> *"Have the gates of death been revealed to you?*
> *Or have you seen the doors of the shadow of death?" (Job 38:17)*

Can you open or close the doors of death, to go in and go out? No.

> *"Where is the way to the dwelling of light?*
> *And darkness, where is its place,*
> *That you may take it to its territory,*
> *That you may know the paths to its home?" (Job 38:19–20)*

What do you know about light and darkness? You may say, light is energy and darkness is the absence of light—but that is not much knowledge. God spoke and there was light. You can't create light. You can only get light from something God already made!

> *"Can you lift up your voice to the clouds,*
> *That an abundance of water may cover you?" (Job 38:34)*

Can you make it rain? No. Our ancient ancestors danced, and it did not rain. Our modern ancestors tried seeding clouds, and that did not work either.

> *"Can you bind the cluster of the Pleiades,*
> *Or loose the belt of Orion?*
> *Can you bring out Mazzaroth [the Constellations] in its season?*

> *Or can you guide the Great Bear [Arcturus] with its cubs?*
> *Do you know the ordinances of the heavens?*
> *Can you set their dominion over the earth?" (Job 38:31–33)*

Do you have any control over the constellations? Can you make them appear to mark the seasons? No.

> *"Does the hawk fly by your wisdom,*
> *And spread its wings toward the south?*
> *Does the eagle mount up at your command,*
> *And make its nest on high?" (Job 39:26–27)*

Did you teach the majestic soaring birds to fly or even how to build a nest in high places? No.

> *"Have you an arm like God?*
> *Or can you thunder with a voice like His?" (Job 40:9)*

Are you as strong as God? Or can you speak with a voice as powerful as thunder? No.

Friends, these are only a few questions to challenge how much we think of ourselves. If we can't do or control any of these little things, how could a human ever think of being or becoming a deity? The wonders of the world around us and the Word of the Lord prove you are not God. What should our response be?

> *Then Job answered the LORD and said:*
> *"I know that You can do everything,*
> *And that no purpose of Yours can be withheld from You...*
> *Therefore I abhor myself,*
> *And repent in dust and ashes." (Job 42:1–2, 6)*

We must acknowledge the Lord is God and give up silly notions of having His power, controlling Him, or making our own rules. Then we can trust God with our lives and enjoy His blessings on Earth and in Heaven.

Think About It

1. Why do people want to be their own bosses?

2. Why is it important to know our limitations?

3. Why is it a good thing that the Lord is God and not us?

Message 21 – I Keep My Promises

Can you trust God? How can you know? If He has shown Himself trustworthy in the past, shouldn't that give confidence to trust now and in the future?

> *The grass withers, the flower fades,*
>   *But the word of our God stands forever. (Isaiah 40:8)*

The beauty of the world around us comes and goes like grass and flowers, but not God's Word. It is sure and steadfast. When the Lord speaks, we can count on it and rely on what He said to be true. Let's prove this by looking at specific promises God made and how He kept them.

Examples of Good Promises

In message six, we saw how God made and kept promises to Abraham. God would later extend the same promise to Abraham's grandson Jacob (Genesis 28). We see how God honored His promise of divine protection when Jacob's scheming uncle was mad at him. His uncle Laban said,

> *"It is in my power to do you harm, but the God of your father spoke to me last night, saying, 'Be careful that you speak to Jacob neither good nor bad.'" (Genesis 31:29)*

The scheming uncle knew he could not touch Jacob because the Lord was with him. God also blessed Jacob with children and wealth as promised.

> *Then Jacob said, "O God of my father Abraham and God of my father Isaac, the LORD who said to me, 'Return to your country and to your family, and I will deal well with you': I am not worthy of the least of all the mercies and of all the truth which You have shown Your servant; for I crossed over this Jordan with my staff, and now I have become two companies." (Genesis 32:9–10)*

Jacob's blessing included the rights to his family's territory. As a young man, he had fled this land with only a staff in his possession, but he returned as the owner of two great groups of flocks and herds (Genesis 32:7).

As another example of God's promises, we see that the Lord pledged to rescue the people of Israel from slavery in Egypt.

> *And the LORD said: "I have surely seen the oppression of My people who are in Egypt, and have heard their cry because of their taskmasters, for I know their sorrows. So I have come down to deliver them out of the hand of the Egyptians, and to bring them up from that land to a good and large land, to a land flowing with milk and honey." (Exodus 3:7–8a)*

Not only did God pledge to deliver the people, He promised to send great judgments on Egypt (Exodus 3:20) and to bring Israel into the promised land. Then the Lord proceeded to show great wonders that we remember as the ten plagues (Exodus 7–12). As promised, God brought His people out of Egypt (Exodus 12:41–42), then led them into the blessed land (see the book of Joshua).

Can You Stop God's Promises?

Even when people don't keep their agreements with God, He keeps His. For example, the Israelites refused to go into the promised land with Moses in Numbers 14. How could God keep His promise then?

> *"Say to them, 'As I live,' says the LORD, 'just as you have spoken in My hearing, so I will do to you: The carcasses of you who have complained against Me shall fall in this wilderness... Except for Caleb the son of Jephunneh and Joshua the son of Nun, you shall by no means enter the land which I swore I would make you dwell in. But your little ones, whom you said would be victims, I will bring in, and they shall know the land which you have despised.'"*
> *(Numbers 14:28–31)*

What happened? They wandered in the desert for 40 years until the rebels who refused God's promise died. Moses took a census at the end of the 40 years. Here are the results.

> *These are those who were numbered by Moses and Eleazar the priest...in the plains of Moab by the Jordan, across from Jericho. But among these there was not a man of those who were numbered by Moses and Aaron the priest...in the Wilderness of Sinai. For the LORD had said of them, "They shall surely die in the wilderness." So there was not left a man of them, except Caleb the son of Jephunneh and Joshua the son of Nun. (Numbers 26:63–65)*

Forty years later, the rebels' children went into the promised land with Joshua. God kept His Word even though people tried to stop Him.

What about this promise from God to Joshua?

> *"Every place that the sole of your foot will tread upon I have given you, as I said to Moses... No man shall be able to stand before you all the days of your life; as I was with Moses, so I will be with you. I will not leave you nor forsake you." (Joshua 1:3, 5)*

The Lord fulfilled that promise, and you can read how He did it in Joshua 6–11. After seeing it all, at the end of his life Joshua testified to his people:

> *"Behold, this day I am going the way of all the earth. And you know in all your hearts and in all your souls that not one thing has failed of all the good things which the LORD your God spoke concerning you. All have come to pass for you; not one word of them has failed." (Joshua 23:14)*

Did you notice the phrase Joshua repeated? God did not leave out one promise. One hundred percent success. What human has a track record like that?

Examples of Judgment Promises

The Lord also makes and keeps promises of judgment. For example, He spoke this word of judgment to Eli, one of His priests:

> *"But now the LORD says: 'Far be it from Me; for those who honor Me I will honor, and those who despise Me shall be lightly esteemed... Now this shall be a sign to you that will come upon your two sons, on Hophni and Phinehas: in one day they shall die, both of them.'" (1 Samuel 2:30b, 34)*

Eli's adult sons Hophni and Phineas were terrible sinners who prevented people from coming to God. As the high priest, Eli should have intervened, but he did not do anything about it. So, when their enemies invaded,

> *Also the ark of God was captured; and the two sons of Eli, Hophni and Phinehas, died. (1 Samuel 4:11)*

As another example, the Lord assured that evil Queen Jezebel would pay for her reign of wickedness.

"The dogs shall eat Jezebel on the plot of ground at Jezreel, and there shall be none to bury her." (2 Kings 9:10)

What happened? A new king took power and found Jezebel looking out of a high window.

Then he said, "Throw her down." So they threw her down, and some of her blood spattered on the wall and on the horses; and he trampled her underfoot. And when he had gone in, he ate and drank. Then he said, "Go now, see to this accursed woman, and bury her, for she was a king's daughter." So they went to bury her, but they found no more of her than the skull and the feet and the palms of her hands. Therefore they came back and told him. And he said, "This is the word of the LORD, which He spoke by His servant Elijah the Tishbite, saying, 'On the plot of ground at Jezreel dogs shall eat the flesh of Jezebel.'" (2 Kings 9:33–36)

Fulfilled Exactly

God doesn't just make promises, He fulfills them exactly. For example, Jesus told His followers,

"But you shall receive power when the Holy Spirit has come upon you; and you shall be witnesses to Me in Jerusalem, and in all Judea and Samaria, and to the end of the earth." (Acts 1:8)

Was this promise fulfilled exactly? Yes, Luke documented how in the book of Acts.

When the Day of Pentecost had fully come, they were all with one accord in one place...
And they were all filled with the Holy Spirit and began to speak with other tongues, as the Spirit gave them utterance. (Acts 2:1, 4)

The Holy Spirit came to live in and empower Jesus' followers, just as He said. They were specifically empowered to speak about Jesus and to do miracles to back up their words. So much so, the religious leaders were amazed.

> *Now when they saw the boldness of Peter and John, and perceived that they were uneducated and untrained men, they marveled. And they realized that they had been with Jesus...*
>
> *[They said], "What shall we do to these men? For, indeed, that a notable miracle has been done through them is evident to all who dwell in Jerusalem, and we cannot deny it." (Acts 4:13, 16)*

These followers did not have prestige or specialized training, yet they boldly told people about Jesus and performed an act that everyone in Jerusalem recognized as a miracle, even the religious leaders who opposed them. That opposition would soon increase.

> *At that time a great persecution arose against the church which was at Jerusalem; and they were all scattered throughout the regions of Judea and Samaria, except the apostles...*
>
> *Therefore those who were scattered went everywhere preaching the word. (Acts 8:1b, 4)*

A great persecution sought to silence the message of Jesus in Jerusalem. However, as Christians fled the city, they spread out and shared the gospel everywhere they went, exactly like Jesus had promised in Acts 1:8.

Confidence

God has a 100 percent record of keeping His promises. Therefore, we can have complete and confident assurance that He meant these wonderful words:

"Whoever believes in Him [Jesus] should not perish but have eternal life." (John 3:15)

"I am with you always, even to the end of the age." (Matthew 28:20b)

These are great promises to rely upon in a world of uncertainty, and there are more to come!

Think About It

1. Why is it important that God kept His promises in the past?

2. What promise may have helped the early Christians in Jerusalem keep their faith when persecution started? (Hint: Matthew 28:20b) How important is that promise?

3. Did this information help with how much you trust God? Why or why not?

Message 22 – I Have Great Promises for You

Now that we know God keeps His promises, what has He promised? As you read through the Bible, you'll come across many examples. However, it is important to realize that not every promise in the Bible is for you. For example, He said,

> *"And I have also given you what you have not asked: both riches and honor, so that there shall not be anyone like you among the kings all your days." (1 Kings 3:13)*

Did God pledge that to everyone? No, He was specifically speaking to Solomon, in answer to a specific prayer, in a specific circumstance. As Dr. McGee used to say, "All Scripture is for us, but not all Scripture is to us."[21]

This means all the Bible has general lessons and blessings for us. However, the specific application of each verse must be found in the context in which it was given. For example, the verses around Solomon's promise show us he was seeking wisdom to be a good leader of God's people (1 Kings 3:7–9). The principle for all of us is that the Lord equips His followers for their mission

---

[21] McGee, Vol. 2, p. 783.

and rewards godly motives (1 Kings 3:10–14).

Solomon's example raises an important issue, especially in light of the rise of the "Prosperity Gospel." Nowhere in the Bible does God promise to make all Christians healthy and wealthy on Earth. Satan wants you to think God is obligated to give you earthly comfort and pleasure, so when these things don't happen, you will lose your faith. Please don't be fooled! Instead, focus on the great things God truly has promised, so you will grow in faith.

All Things

With that in mind, let's see a big promise that the Apostle Peter said is "for" you.

> *His divine power has given to us all things that pertain to life and godliness, through the knowledge of Him who called us by glory and virtue. (2 Peter 1:3)*

The Lord has given us "all things" that we need for godly living. What do you need to live holy?

1. Instructions: God has given His Word (Psalm 119:105).
2. Power: God has given His Holy Spirit (Acts 1:8).
3. Encouragement: God has given Christian friends (Hebrews 10:24–25).
4. A way to call for help: God has given access through prayer (Hebrews 4:16).
5. Understanding: God has given Bible teachers (Colossians 3:16).
6. A place to be refreshed: God has given the local church (Acts 2:46–47).

"All things" is a big promise, so how do we get "all things"? God gives them by His divine power to those who know Him. Remember, the Lord has called every man, woman, boy, and girl to come to Him for new life.

"Look to Me, and be saved,
  All you ends of the earth!
  For I am God, and there is no other." (Isaiah 45:22)

Once we are saved and know the Lord, "all things" are ours. However, you may see some followers of Jesus who don't seem to have "all things." You may feel like you don't have them either. Why might that be?

Imagine a rich relative opened a bank account for you and put $1,000,000 in it. You would have all you need, but if you never went to the bank to access the funds the money would do you no good.

This happens all the time in the spiritual world. If we don't read the Bible, we won't know God's instructions or blessings. If we don't communicate with Jesus' followers, the Christian community can't support us. If we don't pray, we don't give God the opportunity to minister to us. It is not enough to know that the promise of "all things" exists; we must accept the promise and put it to work like the Lord intended.

Precious Promises

His divine power has given to us all things that pertain to life and godliness, through the knowledge of Him who called us by glory and virtue, by which have been given to us exceedingly great and precious promises, that through these you may be partakers of the divine nature, having escaped the corruption that is in the world through lust. (2 Peter 1:3–4)

In addition to "all things," Peter said the Almighty has "given unto us exceedingly great and precious promises." All of God's promises are good, so what is one that is exceedingly great or especially precious? Peter tells us that the special promises allow us to "partake of the divine nature." He is talking about promises of salvation and bringing us into God's family. Here is one example:

> *But as many as received Him, to them He gave the right to become children of God, to those who believe in His name. (John 1:12)*

As we saw before, if we accept Jesus as our Savior, we become children of God. We are born again (John 3:3) into His family. That is a very great promise!

> *Therefore, if anyone is in Christ, he is a new creation; old things have passed away; behold, all things have become new. (2 Corinthians 5:17)*

If we are in Christ (that is, in God's family), we are new people with a new nature. Our old nature with its lusts is no longer our king. This is what Peter means by partaking of the divine nature. Dr. McGee explains,

> *Don't let anybody deceive you into thinking the Christian life is a little series of do's and don'ts—that if you do this and don't do that, you're living the Christian life. Oh, my friend, you are a partaker of the divine nature, the nature of God, and you* want *the things of God.*[22]

What is one thing your divine nature wants? To escape the corruption of the world (2 Peter 3:4). The terrible rottenness of sin bothers your new nature. Before being born again, sin was normal. But now you want freedom from it. God has cleansed your sin and will one day take you to a new clean home that is completely free from sin. If you are tired of sin and its consequences, that is a tremendous promise! While we wait for Heaven,

> *We are ambassadors for Christ, as though God were pleading*

---

[22] McGee, Vol. 5, p. 720.

through us: we implore you on Christ's behalf, be reconciled to God. (2 Corinthians 5:20)

If we are children of God and He has given us of His heavenly nature, we are princes and princesses in Heaven. That means we are ambassadors for Him on Earth. As Jesus' representatives, we live to show how wonderful He is so that others will want to know the Lord. This is why we must know and apply the promises our Father has given us. Otherwise, we will do a poor job of representing Him with human effort.

Think About It

1. Are all the promises in the Bible to us? What tells you if a promise is to you or not?

2. Why is it important not only to know that God has given all things for living holy, but also to access and use them?

3. How would you explain the great and precious promises to someone? Is there anyone you can share that promise with?

Message 23 – The Promise of the Blessed Life

Another of the Lord's wonderful promises for us is a blessed life or happy life.

> *Blessed is the man*
>> *Who walks not in the counsel of the ungodly,*
>> *Nor stands in the path of sinners,*
>> *Nor sits in the seat of the scornful;*
>> *But his delight is in the law of the LORD,*
>> *And in His law he meditates day and night. (Psalm 1:1–2)*

The word translated "blessed" in this passage literally means happy.[23] This happy person does some things and does not do other things. What are these actions?

"Does Not" from Psalm 1:1

A. The happy or blessed person does not walk in the wisdom of ungodly people. Why? The wisdom of this world is foolishness with God.

> *Where is the wise? Where is the scribe? Where is the disputer of*

---

[23] *Strong's* Hebrew definition number 835.

this age? Has not God made foolish the wisdom of this world? (1 Corinthians 1:20)

As we saw in message seven, human wisdom is foolish because it is based on short-sighted things. "Get all you can while you can"; "you only live once"; "if it feels good, do it"—these ideas are indicative of a life that will be wasted in pursuit of that which cannot satisfy, ultimately ending with regret. There is no real or lasting happiness with the ungodly.

B. This person does not stand with sinners.

> *My son, if sinners entice you,*
> *Do not consent...*
> *My son, do not walk in the way with them,*
> *Keep your foot from their path;*
> *For their feet run to evil,*
> *And they make haste to shed blood. (Proverbs 1:10, 15–16)*

We are warned not to associate with sinners because they will entice us to do evil. Once the wrong is done, people live in fear of being caught and in danger of eternal judgment. There is no happiness in such a life.

C. The blessed person does not sit with scorners—those who openly mock God and laugh at the thought of Hell. You can laugh at fire, but it still burns.

> *For the terrible one is brought to nothing,*
> *The scornful one is consumed,*
> *And all who watch for iniquity are cut off. (Isaiah 29:20)*

God said judgment is coming whether you believe it or not. How does the blessed person avoid the judgment and get happiness?

"Does" from Psalm 1:2

A. The blessed person takes delight in God's Word. It is a thing of value, desire, and pleasure.

> *Your words were found, and I ate them,*
> *And Your word was to me the joy and rejoicing of my heart;*
> *For I am called by Your name,*
> *O LORD God of hosts. (Jeremiah 15:16)*

Those who love God's Word have joy. God's Word is like a delicious meal. It causes the heart to rejoice with great satisfaction that sin cannot duplicate. Do you value the Bible? Have you grown to love it? If not yet, how can you?

B. The happy person meditates, contemplates, or thinks about God's Word day and night.

> *"This Book of the Law shall not depart from your mouth, but you*
> *shall meditate in it day and night, that you may observe to do*
> *according to all that is written in it. For then you will make your*
> *way prosperous, and then you will have good success." (Joshua 1:8)*

When you remember what the Lord said and do it, you put yourself on the path of success. This does not mean God has a get-rich-quick program. It does mean you'll be happy pursuing goals that please Him. Why? You'll see and apply God's principles for living. You will avoid temptation and traps. Your obedience has rewards.

Prosperity

> *He shall be like a tree*
> *Planted by the rivers of water,*
> *That brings forth its fruit in its season,*

Whose leaf also shall not wither;
And whatever he does shall prosper. (Psalm 1:3)

As if happiness were not enough, here we see some rewards of delighting in God's Word.

A. The blessed person is like a tree purposely planted. He or she is not tossed just anywhere; notice the Creator is precise in His wise positioning. Planted implies a good foundation so that the storms of life will not easily blow this person over. Jesus said,

> *"Therefore whoever hears these sayings of Mine, and does them, I will liken him to a wise man who built his house on the rock: and the rain descended, the floods came, and the winds blew and beat on that house; and it did not fall, for it was founded on the rock."* *(Matthew 7:24–25)*

Jesus repeated this important principle. Lives built on God's Word will stand. The blessed person is not immune to storms, difficulties, and problems, but the bitter things of life will not ruin this person. That is a comforting assurance.

B. The happy person is near the life-giving water. She is not left to wither in the desert. She has a water supply even if there's no rain, so that the leaves don't wither. Jesus said,

> *"But whoever drinks of the water that I shall give him will never thirst. But the water that I shall give him will become in him a fountain of water springing up into everlasting life." (John 4:14)*

Jesus promised living water to those who follow Him. This water satisfies the soul like nothing else on Earth can.

C. The blessed person is fruitful. His life is not useless. His life is productive. Be sure to recognize that fruitfulness is not instant. Instead, it comes in its season, just as apples take time to grow. Unlike the fake promises of gambling or fast money, this fruit is reliable and delicious.

> *But the fruit of the Spirit is love, joy, peace, longsuffering, kindness, goodness, faithfulness, gentleness, self-control. Against such there is no law. (Galatians 5:22–23)*

God's Spirit produces fruit in our lives also. It is all good fruit—good for us, and good for the people around us. This brings more happiness.

D. Whatever the happy person does prospers. Think of a tree growing, expanding, flourishing.

> *And his [Joseph's] master saw that the LORD was with him and that the LORD made all he did to prosper in his hand. (Genesis 39:3)*

Although Joseph was stolen and sold into slavery, God prospered his work until Pharaoh, king of Egypt, made him ruler of the land (Genesis 41:38–43). There were seriously tough times along the way, but happiness in the end.

The Promise

> *[Jesus said,] "I have come that they may have life, and that they may have it more abundantly. I am the good shepherd." (John 10:10b–11a)*

Jesus is the Good Shepherd and promises life to those who follow Him. What type of life is this? First, it is eternal life as we saw in message twelve. It is also an abundant life (not physical riches). God has blessed us with all spiritual blessings (Ephesians 1:3). This is a happy and blessed life! He even throws in some physical blessings from time to time, according to His divine wisdom. However, we seek the Blesser, not the blessings.

"But seek first the kingdom of God and His righteousness, and all these things shall be added to you." (Matthew 6:33)

Think About It

1. What are three things a blessed (happy) person does not do and why?

2. What are two things a happy person does and why?

3. Does your life resemble "a fruitful tree planted by a river"? If not, what do you think such a life would look like for you?

Message 24 – The Promise of Comfort

In the last message, we saw that even the blessed life is not trouble free. Yet there is good news. God said,

> *"When you pass through the waters, I will be with you;*
> *And through the rivers, they shall not overflow you." (Isaiah 43:2a)*

The Lord promises to be with His people when the river of trouble rages against them.

> *"Be strong and of good courage, do not fear nor be afraid of them; for the LORD your God, He is the One who goes with you. He will not leave you nor forsake you." (Deuteronomy 31:6)*

We can draw on divine strength to face challenges because the Lord is with us. We do not have to be afraid because He will not forsake us. You are never alone. To help us remember that, Jesus gave us promises of comfort for life on Earth.

Peace

> *"These things I have spoken to you, that in Me you may have peace. In the world you will have tribulation; but be of good cheer, I have overcome the world." (John 16:33)*

119

We do not need to have a storm in our minds when a life storm rages around us. We have peace from God. He warned that we would have pain and problems on Earth, so that we would not be caught off-guard or lose heart. And when we struggle to endure, Jesus reminds us that He has conquered the world! That means He is bigger than any trial we could ever face. This is a reason to have "good cheer." Jesus also said,

> *"My sheep hear My voice, and I know them, and they follow Me.*
> *And I give them eternal life, and they shall never perish; neither*
> *shall anyone snatch them out of My hand." (John 10:27–28)*

The Good Shepherd promises eternal security to His sheep. No one can take you out of His hand. Knowing God is with us and we are with Him is the basis of divine comfort. Thus, when Jesus said we will be comforted, we can believe it.

Since Jesus is the Good Shepherd, we can come to Him with our problems and pain as David said:

> *"As for me, I will call upon God,*
> *And the LORD shall save me.*
> *Evening and morning and at noon*
> *I will pray, and cry aloud,*
> *And He shall hear my voice." (Psalm 55:16–17)*

Call on the Lord because He hears and cares.

> *Cast your burden on the LORD,*
> *And He shall sustain you;*
> *He shall never permit the righteous to be moved. (Psalm 55:22)*

Give God your burdens. He is strong enough to carry them even when you are not. In fact, the Lord will sustain you. He does not permit the righteous to be moved, just as we saw the firmly planted tree in Psalm 1.

Comfort Others

Since we have confidence in the Almighty's ability to carry us, we can help others who face sorrow. We have learned the Lord's promises;

> *Therefore comfort one another with these words. (1 Thessalonians 4:18)*

Share God's messages of help and hope with others. Yet don't stop at words; let your actions be a comfort also.

> *Now we exhort you, brethren...comfort the fainthearted, uphold the weak, be patient with all. (1 Thessalonians 5:14)*

You may say, "I'm not strong enough to help someone else with their problems." That's okay, you just share what God has given you.

> *Blessed be the God and Father of our Lord Jesus Christ, the Father of mercies and God of all comfort, who comforts us in all our tribulation, that we may be able to comfort those who are in any trouble, with the comfort with which we ourselves are comforted by God. (2 Corinthians 1:3–4)*

Paul said the Lord is the Father of mercy and God of comfort. This is a great assurance from someone who spoke from experience. Remember, Paul suffered greatly as he traveled to share the gospel. Yet he kept going because the Lord was with him and comforted him. So, these are trustworthy words. Notice that he said God comforts in all tribulation, not just some. And did you see why we have comfort? So we can comfort others with the comfort of God. Again, don't draw from your human strength to help the hurting, but from God's.

God's Ministry of Comfort

In what may be the most famous verse on comfort, Jesus said,

> *"Blessed are those who mourn,*
> *For they shall be comforted." (Matthew 5:4)*

How could Jesus say this? He could say it because He came to comfort.

> *"The Spirit of the Lord is upon Me,*
> *Because He has anointed Me*
> *To preach the gospel to the poor;*
> *He has sent Me to heal the brokenhearted,*
> *To proclaim liberty to the captives*
> *And recovery of sight to the blind,*
> *To set at liberty those who are oppressed." (Luke 4:18)*

Jesus said He came to minister to and rescue the hurting in fulfillment of this prophecy from Isaiah 61:1–2. He did that during His earthly ministry. However, this is only part of the prophecy. It goes on to say,

> *"To proclaim the acceptable year of the LORD,*
> *And the day of vengeance of our God;*
> *To comfort all who mourn,*
> *To console those who mourn in Zion,*
> *To give them beauty for ashes,*
> *The oil of joy for mourning,*
> *The garment of praise for the spirit of heaviness;*
> *That they may be called trees of righteousness,*
> *The planting of the LORD, that He may be glorified." (Isaiah*
> *61:2–3)*

God has not yet finished this comforting ministry. But the Bible describes the day it will be complete:

> *God will wipe away every tear from their eyes; there shall be no more death, nor sorrow, nor crying. There shall be no more pain, for the former things have passed away. (Revelation 21:4)*

We can take comfort knowing that one day there will be no more pain, sorrow, sickness, or death. Until that day, remember this invitation:

> *Let us therefore come boldly to the throne of grace, that we may obtain mercy and find grace to help in time of need. (Hebrews 4:16)*

We can come boldly to the Lord for grace and mercy to get help and hope every day! Our mighty Savior, who holds us in His hand, has promised to provide comfort until we do not need it anymore.

Think About It

1. Why is it important to know the source of comfort? (Hint: credibility and reliability)

2. Besides His love for you, what is another reason God comforts us? (If you need a hint, look at the next question.)

3. What is the basis of our help and comfort for others? (Hint: 1 Thessalonians 4:18)

Message 25 – The Promise to Reward Good Work

In previous messages, we saw that God does a lot for us. However, isn't a relationship supposed to be bidirectional? Don't we have something to do for the Lord? Yes, God has a mission for each of His children, and He rewards our faithfulness when we obey. What is the mission? We saw part of it before, but here is the whole summary.

> *And Jesus came and spoke to them, saying, "All authority has been given to Me in heaven and on earth. Go therefore and make disciples of all the nations, baptizing them in the name of the Father and of the Son and of the Holy Spirit, teaching them to observe all things that I have commanded you; and lo, I am with you always, even to the end of the age." (Matthew 28:18–20)*

Since Jesus has all authority, He has commissioned us to go and tell people about Him. He has promised to be with us on this mission; we are never alone.

Equipped to Work

The Lord has given us His Word to prepare us for the work (2 Timothy 3:16–17). He has given His Holy Spirit to empower and guide us in the work (John 16:13). He has even given us gifts to help with the work.

Having then gifts differing according to the grace that is given to us, let us use them: if prophecy, let us prophesy in proportion to our faith; or ministry, let us use it in our ministering; he who teaches, in teaching; he who exhorts, in exhortation; he who gives, with liberality; he who leads, with diligence; he who shows mercy, with cheerfulness. (Romans 12:6–8)

Notice that God gives different abilities and talents to members of His family. This is not an exhaustive list, but a sample. Some gifts are visible to many, some are for use behind the scenes, but all are for His work. They are all necessary, so don't feel unimportant if your gifts are not for public ministry. This is important to consider because not everyone is a preacher, Bible scholar, or evangelist. In fact, the Lord very specifically did not say everyone was to be a pastor or lead a church. Instead, we have different skills and jobs for a reason.

Use Your Talents Wherever You Are

Imagine, could a "professional" minister come into your workplace and give a sermon? No, but your words and actions at work are a sermon that no preacher can give. Therefore, whatever our vocation or location, we are to look for ways to serve our Savior there. Even Paul the famous missionary used his trade of tent making to pay for his travels (Acts 18:1–3). In fact, Jesus told a parable about using what you have.

"For the kingdom of heaven is like a man traveling to a far country, who called his own servants and delivered his goods to them. And to one he gave five talents, to another two, and to another one, to each according to his own ability; and immediately he went on a journey." (Matthew 25:14–15)

This picture of the kingdom of Heaven illustrates how God has left His children in charge of Earth as stewards. He has divided responsibility based on the abilities He has given to each person.

> *"Then he who had received the five talents went and traded with them, and made another five talents. And likewise he who had received two gained two more also. But he who had received one went and dug in the ground, and hid his lord's money." (Matthew 25:16–18)*

Two servants took their stewardship seriously and put the lord's treasures to work. The third hid what he was entrusted with and did nothing.

> *"After a long time the lord of those servants came and settled accounts with them. So he who had received five talents came and brought five other talents, saying, 'Lord, you delivered to me five talents; look, I have gained five more talents besides them.'" (Matthew 25:19–20)*

At the appointed time, the stewards were called to give account. Two used their abilities to grow their lord's treasures and were commended and rewarded. They were recognized for being faithful and entrusted with rulership. As if that were not enough, they were privileged to share in the lord's joy (Matthew 25:21, 23). What about the third servant?

> *"Then he who had received the one talent came and said, 'Lord, I knew you to be a hard man, reaping where you have not sown, and gathering where you have not scattered seed. And I was afraid, and went and hid your talent in the ground. Look, there you have what is yours.'*
>
> *"But his lord answered and said to him, 'You wicked and lazy servant, you knew that I reap where I have not sown, and gather where I have not scattered seed. So you ought to have deposited my money with the bankers, and at my coming I would have received*

back my own with interest."' (Matthew 25:24–27)

He was condemned as wicked and lazy for not using his brain. Regardless of his management skills, his lord said he could at least have earned interest from the bank. Thus, we see the Lord will reward the faithful and condemn the lazy.

Rewards Coming

What talents and abilities do you have? Have you identified a spiritual gift that God has given? Consider, are you being a good steward of such things so that the Lord will reward you?

> *[He] "will render to each one according to his deeds": eternal life to those who by patient continuance in doing good seek for glory, honor, and immortality; but to those who are self-seeking and do not obey the truth, but obey unrighteousness—indignation and wrath, tribulation and anguish, on every soul of man who does evil...but glory, honor, and peace to everyone who works what is good. (Romans 2:6–10a)*

The certainty of a date for reward and judgment is an important theme in the Bible. God loves His children and often reminds us to do good so we can be rewarded. Here, He specifically mentions those who are "patient...in doing good" and promises "glory, honor, and peace to everyone who works what is good."

We should also notice the wrath and anguish that will befall those souls who do evil. God does not want that to happen to anyone (1 Timothy 2:4). This is why He gave the mission of sharing Jesus' message of salvation. Knowing that we have love from God should motivate us to share it, but the Lord has given extra incentive by blessing us for doing our job!

Therefore, my beloved brethren, be steadfast, immovable, always abounding in the work of the Lord, knowing that your labor is not in vain in the Lord. (1 Corinthians 15:58)

Having the promises of God, we can be sure in our faith and faithful in our work. In fact, we are to abound in working for our Lord, knowing He will reward us.

He specifically said, "Your labor is not in vain in the Lord." However, we don't always see the result of our labor in this life. Paul said,

"I planted, Apollos watered, but God gave the increase. So then neither he who plants is anything, nor he who waters, but God who gives the increase. Now he who plants and he who waters are one, and each one will receive his own reward according to his own labor." (1 Corinthians 3:6–8)

The famous apostle compared working for the Almighty to farming. He planted, someone else watered, but God provided the harvest at the right time. So, your good work, your spiritual conversation with someone needing Jesus, or even an invitation to Bible study can be part of the process. You may not know if you are planting, watering, weeding, or about to collect fruit. The important thing is to be faithful, as you see the promise of a reward was mentioned again.

And let us not grow weary while doing good, for in due season we shall reap if we do not lose heart. Therefore, as we have opportunity, let us do good to all, especially to those who are of the household of faith. (Galatians 6:9–10)

When you don't see flowers or fruit on a plant, it is easy to get tired of working in a field. However, we are encouraged to keep at it. Why? The harvest will come; the Lord will reward His faithful children!

Think About It

1. What is the overarching mission that God has given His children? Even if you are not the pastor of a church, how can you contribute to this mission?

2. Why does the Lord reward His people for good work?

3. Why is the promise of a reward important for you?

Message 26 – The Promise to Hear Prayers

Have you ever prayed and wondered if God heard or cared? After seeing the previous messages, you know He cares, but does He hear? The Bible tells us to pray, so why doesn't God answer? Let's see what Jesus said about this.

> *Then He spoke a parable to them, that men always ought to pray and not lose heart, saying: "There was in a certain city a judge who did not fear God nor regard man. Now there was a widow in that city; and she came to him, saying, 'Get justice for me from my adversary.' And he would not for a while; but afterward he said within himself, 'Though I do not fear God nor regard man, yet because this widow troubles me I will avenge her, lest by her continual coming she weary me.'"*
>
> *Then the Lord said, "Hear what the unjust judge said. And shall God not avenge His own elect who cry out day and night to Him, though He bears long with them? I tell you that He will avenge them speedily. Nevertheless, when the Son of Man comes, will He really find faith on the earth?" (Luke 18:1–8)*

What is Jesus teaching us in this parable? First, if a crooked judge will give justice just so someone will stop bothering him, don't you think the Lord who loves you will do right? Second, sometimes God lets His children wait to get what they want. While waiting, we should not stop crying out to our

Father. Third, God hears His elect, those who are His children. He is not obligated to hear people outside His family. Finally, there is an element of faith involved with prayer. Jesus is wondering if He will see faith when you pray. Let's examine these concepts.

A. The Lord will take care of his followers.

> *"Because he has set his love upon Me, therefore I will deliver him;*
> *I will set him on high, because he has known My name.*
> *He shall call upon Me, and I will answer him;*
> *I will be with him in trouble;*
> *I will deliver him and honor him." (Psalm 91:14–15)*

God is with those who love Him. He hears when they call, and He delivers. He can deliver from trouble or through trouble (Hebrews 11:32–38).

B. Sometimes the Lord will make us wait. That does not mean He has not heard.

> *Therefore the sisters sent to Him, saying, "Lord, behold, he whom You love is sick."*
> *When Jesus heard that, He said, "This sickness is not unto death, but for the glory of God, that the Son of God may be glorified through it."*
> *Now Jesus loved Martha and her sister and Lazarus. So, when He heard that he was sick, He stayed two more days in the place where He was. (John 11:3, 5-6)*

Jesus loved these people who requested healing for their brother. Yet He delayed in going to help. When he arrived, Lazarus had been dead four days (John 11:17). You probably know the story. The family was devastated and did not understand Jesus' delay. However, we begin to get insight when

Jesus said to her, "Did I not say to you that if you would believe you would see the glory of God?" (John 11:40)

Jesus let us know the delay in answering the request was for the glory of God; it was not because He didn't hear. Then He raised Lazarus from the dead (John 11:43–44).

C. God always hears His children.

> *The eyes of the LORD are on the righteous,*
> *And His ears are open to their cry.*
> *The face of the LORD is against those who do evil,*
> *To cut off the remembrance of them from the earth. (Psalm 34:15–16)*

As a Father, it is God's delight to hear and help His family. He always watches over them. However, He is against those who are against Him. Remember from message two, all humans are against the Lord because we are born sinners. However, our Creator wants everyone to be in His family; that is why He sent Jesus to rescue us. Therefore, the Lord will always hear one specific prayer from a sinner.

> *For "whoever calls on the name of the Lord shall be saved." (Romans 10:13)*

God may not hear a sinner's prayer for a job, health, or happiness, but the Almighty has promised to save whoever comes to Him (Matthew 11:28). After they come, God hears all their prayers.

D. You must have faith when you pray.

> *And whatever things you ask in prayer, believing, you will receive. (Matthew 21:22)*

Jesus said that when you pray, believe that God hears and answers. James further explained,

> *If any of you lacks wisdom, let him ask of God, who gives to all liberally and without reproach, and it will be given to him. But let him ask in faith, with no doubting, for he who doubts is like a wave of the sea driven and tossed by the wind. For let not that man suppose that he will receive anything from the Lord. (James 1:5–7)*

This specific example is praying for wisdom. However, the principle applies broadly. If you doubt God, don't expect to receive anything. Why not?

> *But without faith it is impossible to please Him, for he who comes to God must believe that He is, and that He is a rewarder of those who diligently seek Him. (Hebrews 11:6)*

The Lord is pleased with faith. In fact, He rewards it. If that is true, why don't we always get what we request?

Three Answers to Prayer

It has been said that the Lord answers prayer in three ways: yes, no, and wait. We have discussed waiting already, so why does He sometimes answer yes and sometimes no?

> *Every good gift and every perfect gift is from above, and comes down from the Father of lights, with whom there is no variation or shadow of turning. (James 1:17)*

The Lord gives good and perfect gifts. Since He knows the consequences of everything on Earth and in eternity, He does what is best for His children. Since we have limited knowledge, we often can't tell what is best. However, *we know that all things work together for good to those who love God, to those who are the called according to His purpose. (Romans 8:28)*

Therefore, if the answer of yes is good for you, that is what you will get (John 15:7). If the answer of no is better, God will say it (James 4:3).

Sometimes people will say if you have more faith, the Lord will give what you want. That is simply not true. In fact, Jesus taught that you only need a little faith (Matthew 17:20) for God to act. If the size of our faith doesn't affect God's ability or willingness to act, why do we need faith at all? First, you need faith to know that God can give or do. Then you need to have faith that He will do what is best. And it takes faith to trust that the Lord loves you if He says no. As Jesus prayed,

> *"Father, if it is Your will, take this cup away from Me; nevertheless not My will, but Yours, be done." (Luke 22:42)*

Jesus did not get what He asked for, but He trusted the will of God the Father was best. All this leads to an important question. When you pray, are you praying for God's will or your will to be done? The Lord invites us to talk about everything with Him because He cares about all aspects of our lives (1 Peter 5:7). However, when you ask, are you asking for things that will bring glory to God or to you?

Think About It

1. Whose prayer does God always hear? Why?

2. Why is it important to have faith when you pray?

3. Why does the Lord say no to our prayers sometimes? Do you think it takes more faith for an answer of yes or no?

Message 27 – Pray for Others

In the previous message, we learned that the Lord always hears His children's prayers. Therefore, when Jesus gave instructions to pray, we can have confidence that God will help. He said,

> *"Watch and pray, lest you enter into temptation. The spirit indeed is willing, but the flesh is weak." (Matthew 26:41)*

Jesus addressed a very important reason to pray for ourselves—so we can resist temptation. Paul echoed this while discussing the armor of God that we need to fight the devil. He said,

> *"[Pray] always with all prayer and supplication in the Spirit, being watchful to this end with all perseverance and supplication for all the saints." (Ephesians 6:18)*

We are to pray continually for ourselves and others to be victorious in fighting Satan and his schemes. Thus, it is evident that prayer is critical for followers of Jesus—but what should we be praying?

What to Pray

Until now, we talked primarily about praying for self, but Paul talks about praying for others. In message fourteen, we briefly looked at this verse, but let's consider it from a different point of view.

Therefore I exhort first of all that supplications, prayers, interces-
sions, and giving of thanks be made for all men, for kings and all
who are in authority. (1 Timothy 2:1–2a)

Paul urges us to pray for others as a top priority. He is specific in the types
of prayer as well.

1. We are to make supplications to God. That means to petition our
   heavenly Father for someone's needs.
2. Paul used the word "prayers" in association with earnest prayer.[24] Like
   Elijah, we are to pray seriously and powerfully for others.
3. He said to intercede—that means to go on another person's behalf to
   mediate or gain favor. We should pray that people will be reconciled to
   God.
4. Finally, we are to give thanks for others. When is the last time you told
   God "Thank you" for a politician, coworker, the police, or even your
   boss?

Paul said we are to pray for all people, not just our family and friends. He
specifically called out rulers and authorities as people in need of prayer.
When you think about the list of types of prayer, it makes sense that we
should plead with the Almighty that our leaders would seek His wisdom.
Why are we to pray these things?

That we may lead a quiet and peaceable life in all godliness and
reverence. For this is good and acceptable in the sight of God
our Savior, who desires all men to be saved and to come to the
knowledge of the truth. (1 Timothy 2:2b–4)

We pray for others so that we can lead peaceful lives, showing godliness and
honesty. How is that logical? Shouldn't we just pray for a peaceful life? No,

---

[24] *Strong's* Greek definition number 4335.

the point of your peaceful life is to help others know Jesus.

If you pray for a neighbor who is an alcoholic, you will think twice about having alcohol when you invite him to a cookout. That way he can see a difference in your life. When you pray for a coworker, you will think twice about gossiping so there will be credibility inviting her to church. When you pray for unpopular elected officials, you will think twice before bashing them in public. That way you can obey the command,

> *Let no corrupt word proceed out of your mouth, but what is good*
> *for necessary edification, that it may impart grace to the hearers.*
> *(Ephesians 4:29)*

Your obedience will help people listen to the good words you speak; your words can then impact lives.

We pray for others' spiritual and physical well-being in preparation for and as part of our mission to help them know Jesus. Praying for them not only brings God's influence into their lives, but it changes our conduct so we can be God's influence! This is "good and acceptable" in God's sight, because He "desires all men to be saved."

Have you noticed a theme in these messages from Heaven? The Lord isn't talking just to hear Himself speak. He is calling every man, woman, boy, and girl so they can get to Heaven! Therefore, our prayers and actions should help get that message out. But what do we pray for after people come to know the Lord? Paul gave us an idea in the prayers he recorded for followers of Jesus:

> *That the God of our Lord Jesus Christ, the Father of glory, may*
> *give to you the spirit of wisdom and revelation in the knowledge of*
> *Him, the eyes of your understanding being enlightened; that you*
> *may know what is the hope of His calling, what are the riches of*

137

the glory of His inheritance in the saints, and what is the exceeding greatness of His power toward us who believe, according to the working of His mighty power. (Ephesians 1:17–19)

Paul set an example by requesting specific and potent blessings for Christians.

A. He asked the Lord to give his friends the spirit of wisdom and reveal knowledge about Jesus with understanding. We need wisdom to live godly lives and avoid temptation. We need knowledge of Jesus to rely on His power. We need to understand what we see and hear to put things in proper spiritual perspective.

B. Paul prayed that they would know the hope of God's calling. As followers of Jesus, we have great hope in Him who has called us to be saved. This is a hope of certainty. Lon Solomon, the famous former pastor of McLean Bible Church in Virginia used to say, "This is not a 'hope so' hope. It's a 'know so' hope!" We don't hope we are going to Heaven, instead we know it because of Jesus' promise. Part of the promise is a glorious inheritance. Having this hope for the future changes how we live today.

C. He prayed that believers would know the exceeding greatness of God's power for them. We need to know and trust the Lord's mighty power. When we truly believe He is the Almighty, we discover an eagerness to share that knowledge of Him:

God has not given us a spirit of fear, but of power and of love and of a sound mind. (2 Timothy 1:7)

God has given His power, love, and soundness of mind to us. These gifts are for His work. Therefore, we do not have to fear. Start praying for the people around you. And let them see how the Lord's power gave you a new life and hope for eternity.

Think About It

1. Often we pray for our physical needs, but what did Jesus tell us to pray about in Matthew 26:41?

2. What are two reasons we pray for "all men" or all people? (Hint: one reason deals with you and the other deals with God.)

3. What types of things should we pray for followers of Jesus?

Message 28 – Care for the Needy

Many times, people associate doing good things and helping the poor with Christianity, and they should. However, sometimes we have a problem that hinders good work. In fact, we are told,

> *If anyone among you thinks he is religious, and does not bridle his tongue but deceives his own heart, this one's religion is useless. Pure and undefiled religion before God and the Father is this: to visit orphans and widows in their trouble, and to keep oneself unspotted from the world. (James 1:26–27)*

If you don't control your tongue, then your gossip, cursing, mean words, dirty jokes, half-truths and outright lies will tell others you're not really a follower of Jesus. It should tell you the same thing! Your religion is useless if it does not lead to self-control.

Worthwhile religion shows how your heart is right with God. You demonstrate God's heart to the world by caring for people, especially the vulnerable and needy, and by exhibiting a lifestyle that is not stained by society's sins.

Commanded to Care?

We saw in previous messages that the Lord really cares about us. So, it should not be surprising that He wants us to care about people also. The Bible records many instances of God commanding His people to provide for and protect widows, fatherless children, and strangers (people of different ethnic groups or nationalities).

> *"You shall neither mistreat a stranger nor oppress him, for you were strangers in the land of Egypt.*
> *"You shall not afflict any widow or fatherless child." (Exodus 22:21-22)*

Not only were the Israelites told to protect these people, God said to love them (Deuteronomy 10:19). He also commanded a charity program.

> *"At the end of every third year you shall bring out the tithe of your produce of that year and store it up within your gates. And the Levite, because he has no portion nor inheritance with you, and the stranger and the fatherless and the widow who are within your gates, may come and eat and be satisfied, that the LORD your God may bless you in all the work of your hand which you do." (Deuteronomy 14:28-29)*

The people were to give ten percent of their crops to the poor every three years. At religious festivals, the poor were to be fed (Deuteronomy 16:10–11). Also, during harvest of any crop, the poor were allowed to glean the fields so they could eat (Deuteronomy 24:19–22).

The Bible also shows the Almighty sending people to help the poor. You might remember the story of Ruth and how Boaz rescued her from widowhood and poverty. During a famine, the Lord sent Elijah the prophet to help a widow and her son (1 Kings 17:8–16). Even Jesus took time to help a widow whose only son had died.

> *When the Lord saw her, He had compassion on her and said to her, "Do not weep." Then He came and touched the open coffin, and those who carried him stood still. And He said, "Young man, I say*

to you, arise." So he who was dead sat up and began to speak. And
He presented him to his mother. (Luke 7:13–15)

This lady needed her son to provide for her in the world of ancient economics, and Jesus has compassion on her.

Compassion for God?

We saw before that when Jesus returns to Earth, He will reward care for the oppressed and poor as having been done for Him (Matthew 25:31–40). This is an important concept we should not rush by. Showing compassion for others is a form of loving the Lord:

> *He who has pity on the poor lends to the LORD,*
> *And He will pay back what he has given. (Proverbs 19:17)*

Can you imagine giving God a loan? Unlike people, God always keeps His promises, so He will pay all obligations. In fact, Jesus said,

> *"Give, and it will be given to you: good measure, pressed down,*
> *shaken together, and running over will be put into your bosom.*
> *For with the same measure that you use, it will be measured back*
> *to you." (Luke 6:38)*

This knowledge should change our priorities, shifting from a focus on self to concern for others, as the Lord intends.

As an example, consider how the early church understood the importance of caring for others.

> *Now all who believed were together, and had all things in common,*
> *and sold their possessions and goods, and divided them among all,*
> *as anyone had need. (Acts 2:44–45)*

Be careful to see what this verse does and does not say. It does not say the government redistributed the peoples' wealth. It did not say the masses took from the rich to give to the poor. Giving away someone else's possessions is not compassion. It did say believers in Jesus saw needs and had true compassion to meet those needs of their own free will with their own money. Their faith led to action.

> *So continuing daily with one accord in the temple, and breaking bread from house to house, they ate their food with gladness and simplicity of heart, praising God and having favor with all the people. And the Lord added to the church daily those who were being saved. (Acts 2:46–47)*

Notice, daily they had spiritual fellowship. They praised the Lord and were viewed favorably by the people. Why? The masses saw that faith in Jesus resulted in genuine care for others which impacted the city. This led many of them to believe also.

Faith in Action

Through the years that the Christian church has been in existence, it has brought glory to God by caring for the needy. Here are some examples to consider.

In the ancient world, the lives of children had no value. Infants were sacrificed to devils (Deuteronomy 12:31). We know that Romans abandoned unwanted babies, leaving them to die of exposure.[25] However, Christians began to rescue these babies and eventually founded orphanages to care for children in desperate need.[26] Why? God said help the helpless.

---

[25] George Grant, *Third Time Around: A History of the Pro-Life Movement from the First Century to the Present*, p.20, Legacy, Franklin, Tennessee 1991, 1994.

[26] D. James Kennedy, *What if Jesus Had Never Been Born?*, p.12 Thomas Nelson Publishers 1994.

Prior to Christianity, sick people had little hope or help unless they were rich. They were driven out or abandoned (1 Samuel 30:13). "But hospitals as we know them began through the influence of Christianity. The love and example of Jesus Christ inspired a new attitude toward helping the ill."[27]

When it comes to caring for the poor, Dr. James Kennedy argues that "the church of Jesus Christ has done more—and often still does more—than any other institution in history to alleviate poverty. Furthermore, it has set a pattern for relief [that] has been copied worldwide."[28]

Friend, what reason does the world have to believe us when we tell them of Jesus? They need to see action:

> *"By this all will know that you are My disciples, if you have love for one another." (John 13:35)*

Think About It

1. How did James describe a worthwhile religion?

2. Why do you think the Lord cares about the poor and hurting so much?

3. What are some ways you can begin to show compassion?

---

[27] Ibid, p.144.

[28] Ibid, p. 28.

Message 29 – Learn My Word

Although we are looking at 30 specific messages from Heaven, there are many more things God has to say, and they're all found in the Bible. Why did God give us that amazing book? First, we must know this truth:

All Scripture is given by inspiration of God. (2 Timothy 3:16a)

It is critical that we recognize that Scripture, or the Bible as we call it, is God's Word. He had humans write it down, but the words are His (2 Peter 1:21). Please remember that one person's words are no better than any others. We do not rely on human words but God's because His words are

profitable for doctrine, for reproof, for correction, for instruction in righteousness. (2 Timothy 3:16b)

Only the Lord's words have the power to make us wise about faith and salvation in Jesus (Romans 1:16). Remember, human constructs of religion are worthless, as we saw in message ten. The Bible is the standard by which we know truth from error (John 17:17). Therefore, we rely on the word of the Lord. Again,

All Scripture is given by inspiration of God, and is profitable for doctrine, for reproof, for correction, for instruction in righteousness, that the man of God may be complete, thoroughly equipped for every good work. (2 Timothy 3:16–17)

145

The Bible is profitable; it is valuable and brings good things. What are the benefits?

1. It is profitable for doctrine—the fundamentals and basis of faith.
2. It is profitable for reproof—evidence or admonition against wrong. (Keep in mind, the Almighty makes the rules, not us. He declares what is right and wrong.)
3. It is profitable for correction to make sure we don't stray from the path of truth.
4. It is profitable for instruction, teaching us how to live in righteousness.

Thus, we see the Bible is potent and very useful, but is there a specific reason why we need it?

Why Do We Need the Bible?

The Lord gave us His Word so that followers of Jesus would be complete and fully equipped. Without the Bible we are incomplete, lacking, and unable to fully live. We need it to do God's work. We need it to do good work. We need it to live rightly, since we live by His power, not human power.

The Bible is of utmost importance for a Christian, which is why Satan tries to keep you from reading, learning, studying, and sharing it (Ephesians 6:12, 2 Timothy 3:8, 2 Corinthians 4:4).

> *Put on the whole armor of God, that you may be able to stand against the wiles of the devil. (Ephesians 6:11)*

The Lord has given us spiritual armor to protect against Satan's attacks and the "sword of the Spirit, which is the word of God" to fight back (Ephesians 6:14–17). The Bible is our spiritual weapon to fight the devil. Jesus showed us this when He was tested. For every temptation Satan brought, Jesus defeated it by quoting the Bible (Matthew 4:1–11). Jesus could have blasted Satan, but He chose to fight using the Bible, setting an example for us. It is truly an amazing book. Let's look at more of its power.

> *How can a young man cleanse his way?*
> *By taking heed according to Your word. (Psalm 119:9)*

God's Word has the power to cleanse us.

> *Your word I have hidden in my heart,*
> *That I might not sin against You. (Psalm 119:11)*

Scripture has the power to keep us from sin; that is, it can keep us clean.

> *My soul clings to the dust;*
> *Revive me according to Your word. (Psalm 119:25)*

What the Almighty has spoken has power to revive our souls.

> *Incline my heart to Your testimonies,*
> *And not to covetousness. (Psalm 119:36)*

The Lord's testimonies have the power to protect us from greed.

> *Let Your mercies come also to me, O LORD—*
> *Your salvation according to Your word. (Psalm 119:41)*

God's Word brings salvation.

> *This is my comfort in my affliction,*
> *For Your word has given me life. (Psalm 119:50)*

The Bible brings comfort in affliction.

I have more understanding than all my teachers,
    For Your testimonies are my meditation. (Psalm 119:99)

Scripture gives wisdom and understanding to those who meditate on it.

Your word is a lamp to my feet
    And a light to my path. (Psalm 119:105)

The Bible is a light to guide us in a dark world.

Value vs Time

The Bible is truly a remarkable book, one to be desired and studied. This is why Moses said of God's Word,

> *"And these words which I command you today shall be in your heart. You shall teach them diligently to your children, and shall talk of them when you sit in your house, when you walk by the way, when you lie down, and when you rise up." (Deuteronomy 6:6–7)*

These verses command us to teach the next generation what the Lord has spoken. However, we can't teach what we do not know. Therefore, it is vital to store God's Word in our hearts; that is, we have to study and memorize it. This principle is so important that the Bible repeats it often.

> *Let the word of Christ dwell in you richly in all wisdom, teaching and admonishing one another in psalms and hymns and spiritual songs, singing with grace in your hearts to the Lord. (Colossians 3:16)*

The Lord's Word is to live in us so we can share it with others. Putting time into reading and learning the Bible will take effort. It is work, but work you can enjoy if you put it in proper perspective. Just as the gardener enjoys the labor and sweat because there is joy and satisfaction in the produce, the Bible student can enjoy studying. Yet beyond that, when we realize our Creator's Word is a special gift from Heaven, we will treasure it and want to spend time with it.

> *I rejoice at Your word*
> *As one who finds great treasure. (Psalm 119:162)*

Therefore, ask God to give you an appetite for the Bible (Psalm 119:103) and pray,

> *Open my eyes, that I may see*
> *Wondrous things from Your law. (Psalm 119:18)*

Think About It

1. What are some reasons it is important for you to learn what God has said?

2. What are some powers, benefits, and blessings that come from the Bible?

3. How can you cultivate an appetite for God's Word? (Hint: your habits and preferences are influenced by how and where you spend your time.)

Message 30 – I'm Coming Back to Earth

Did you know that Jesus is coming back to Earth? God told us about Jesus' first coming all through the Old Testament. This is the Christmas we celebrate today, the day when He came as our Savior. Although there were hints in the Old Testament, we are clearly told throughout the New Testament that Jesus will come again. Let's investigate this message beginning with His departure from the planet.

> *Therefore, when they had come together, they asked Him, saying, "Lord, will You at this time restore the kingdom to Israel?" And He said to them, "It is not for you to know times or seasons which the Father has put in His own authority. But you shall receive power when the Holy Spirit has come upon you; and you shall be witnesses to Me in Jerusalem, and in all Judea and Samaria, and to the end of the earth."*
>
> *Now when He had spoken these things, while they watched, He was taken up, and a cloud received Him out of their sight. (Acts 1:6–9)*

After Jesus paid for our sins and rose from the dead, the disciples asked if He was ready to set up an earthly kingdom. He said the timing of the kingdom was not for them to know. Instead, they were to share His message. Then Jesus left for Heaven. They were perplexed.

> *And while they looked steadfastly toward heaven as He went up,*

behold, two men stood by them in white apparel, who also said,
"Men of Galilee, why do you stand gazing up into heaven? This
same Jesus, who was taken up from you into heaven, will so come
in like manner as you saw Him go into heaven." (Acts 1:10–11)

This is a bit humorous. You can imagine Jesus in Heaven looking down and thinking, "Will they stand there all day?" So, He sent two angels with a message: "Jesus is coming back one day."

Why Is Jesus Coming Back?

The Lord had told the disciples about His future return before, but they did not understand.

"For the Son of Man will come in the glory of His Father with
His angels, and then He will reward each according to his works."
(Matthew 16:27)

Jesus said He was coming again to judge and reward. Notice the contrast to His first coming, where His mission was to seek and save. Also, unlike the first coming, His return will be a surprise. Jesus said,

"Watch therefore, for you do not know what hour your Lord is
coming. But know this, that if the master of the house had known
what hour the thief would come, he would have watched and not
allowed his house to be broken into. Therefore you also be ready, for
the Son of Man is coming at an hour you do not expect." (Matthew
24:42–44)

We do not know when Jesus is coming back. We just know that He is, and that we must be ready. How can we be ready? What does it mean to watch for Jesus? Consider what Jesus said:

"Who then is a faithful and wise servant, whom his master made ruler over his household, to give them food in due season? Blessed is that servant whom his master, when he comes, will find so doing. Assuredly, I say to you that he will make him ruler over all his goods." (Matthew 24:45–47)

To help us be ready, Jesus gave the illustration of a servant who was put in charge of a household. The servant was to do his job faithfully until the ruler of the house returned. Then he would be blessed. Similarly, Jesus left us, His followers, as stewards with a mission. We are to do His will and work until He returns. The entire time we are faithful, we are ready and can watch with joyful expectation.

Knowing that Jesus will return to reward people and judge the unrighteous should be a great motivator. We get this impression because the Lord talked about it a lot. For example,

"For as the lightning comes from the east and flashes to the west, so also will the coming of the Son of Man be." (Matthew 24:27)

"Watch therefore, for you know neither the day nor the hour in which the Son of Man is coming." (Matthew 25:13)

"When the Son of Man comes in His glory, and all the holy angels with Him, then He will sit on the throne of His glory." (Matthew 25:31)

"Jesus said to him, 'It is as you said. Nevertheless, I say to you, hereafter you will see the Son of Man sitting at the right hand of the Power, and coming on the clouds of heaven.'" (Matthew 26:64)

"And if I go and prepare a place for you, I will come again and

receive you to Myself; that where I am, there you may be also."
(John 14:3)

Though we don't know the day Jesus is coming back, we are to live as if it could be today. This was the expectation of the early church.

For you yourselves know perfectly that the day of the Lord so comes as a thief in the night. (1 Thessalonians 5:2)

They were looking for Jesus, and so should we.

Therefore be patient, brethren, until the coming of the Lord. See how the farmer waits for the precious fruit of the earth, waiting patiently for it until it receives the early and latter rain. You also be patient. Establish your hearts, for the coming of the Lord is at hand. (James 5:7–8)

As James told the church, the Lord is coming, and His coming is near. Therefore, we are to wait patiently as a farmer tending the fields with expectations for the harvest.

Great Motivation

Jesus didn't have to tell us He would return, so why did He?

For the grace of God that brings salvation has appeared to all men, teaching us that, denying ungodliness and worldly lusts, we should live soberly, righteously, and godly in the present age, looking for the blessed hope and glorious appearing of our great God and Savior Jesus Christ. (Titus 2:11–13)

He wants to motivate us to live righteously. He also wants us to have hope, a special hope, even in a world of sadness. There's also another reason.

I charge you therefore before God and the Lord Jesus Christ, who will judge the living and the dead at His appearing and His kingdom: Preach the word! Be ready in season and out of season. Convince, rebuke, exhort, with all longsuffering and teaching. (2 Timothy 4:1-2)

Remember, Jesus is coming back to judge the world. We are to warn people so they can escape the terrible judgment:

The Lord Jesus [will be] revealed from heaven with His mighty angels, in flaming fire taking vengeance on those who do not know God, and on those who do not obey the gospel of our Lord Jesus Christ. These shall be punished with everlasting destruction from the presence of the Lord and from the glory of His power, when He comes, in that Day, to be glorified in His saints and to be admired among all those who believe. (2 Thessalonians 1:7b-10a)

Jesus is not coming again as a humble baby in a manger, but as a mighty King with an army to execute vengeance on sinners and rebels. This will be a terrifying experience for unbelievers.

"Then the sign of the Son of Man will appear in heaven, and then all the tribes of the earth will mourn, and they will see the Son of Man coming on the clouds of heaven with power and great glory." (Matthew 24:30)

His second coming is to be a great motivator. It gives hope for the future when days are dark. It encourages us to be faithful in our love for God and our mission. It should make us afraid for neighbors who do not know Jesus. We are to be so afraid for them that we warn people, "Come to Jesus and leave your sin." That is the point of all the messages from Heaven—to get you and everyone you know to enter into the joy of the Lord while you are on Earth and into God's home when it's time to leave this world.

Think About It

1. The idea of dying one day in the far-off future and seeing Jesus is a comforting thought. What difference does it make in your thinking to know He could come back to Earth today?

2. Why do you think Jesus did not say exactly when He would return? Might you wait until the last minute to get ready if He did?

3. We are to tell people Jesus came to rescue them from sin because He said to do it. How does knowing the fate of sinners give you extra motivation?

Conclusion – The Ultimate Message

It is amazing that the Almighty, the Creator of the universe, the Lord Himself wants to talk with a single small creature—you! He went through a lot of trouble to reveal, say, record, and preserve His messages from Heaven in a Book of books, the Bible. Hopefully, you have been inspired and challenged as you investigated these messages. They are precious and powerful, sure and steadfast, time-tested and true.

> *Therefore we must give the more earnest heed to the things we have heard, lest we drift away. For if the word spoken through angels proved steadfast, and every transgression and disobedience received a just reward,* <u>*how shall we escape if we neglect so great a salvation,*</u> *which at the first began to be spoken by the Lord [Jesus], and was confirmed to us by those who heard Him, God also bearing witness both with signs and wonders, with various miracles, and gifts of the Holy Spirit, according to His own will?* (**Hebrews 2:1–4** *emphasis added*)

This is a warning and reminder about the messages from Heaven. Believe, apply, and share God's Word because of the ultimate message, "How shall we escape if we neglect so great a salvation?" Throughout the Old Testament, patriarchs, angels, and prophets delivered messages about the arrival of a Savior. Then Jesus came and brought the message of salvation. He even sent His apostles to spread the message and do miracles as proof. God did all of that work because *there is no escape if we reject Jesus.*

So, the most important question becomes, what will you do with Jesus? If you need help to be certain, please read Appendix A – How to Get to Heaven. If you know Jesus is your Savior, please see Appendix B – Resources to Keep Listening.

If this book has been helpful, please share it with a friend. Also, posting a review on Amazon will help others find the book so it can encourage them. Of course, I'd like to know your thoughts, as well. The *About the Author* page at the end tells how to connect with me.

Appendix A – How to Get to Heaven

We all have a very big problem: no one is good enough to get to Heaven because we all sin. What is sin? Sin is anything we think, say, or do that disobeys God. You might say, "Why should I worry about disobeying God?" The problem is that sin separates us from God and keeps us out of Heaven when we die.

> *For the wages of sin is death, but the gift of God is eternal life in Christ Jesus our Lord. (Romans 6:23)*

Sin has a penalty, which is death—not just physical, but spiritual as well. You've heard of Hell; that is the place where all sinners are destined to spend eternity and experience spiritual death. The Lord doesn't send people to Hell, we send ourselves by choosing to sin. But God offers eternal life.

The good news is that God doesn't want anyone to go to Hell.

> *The Lord is not slack concerning His promise, as some count slackness, but is longsuffering toward us, not willing that any should perish but that all should come to repentance. (2 Peter 3:9)*

God wants all humans to repent (that is, turn from sin) so that no one would perish in Hell. This is where Jesus enters the picture.

> *"For God so loved the world that He gave His only begotten Son, that whoever believes in Him should not perish but have everlasting life." (John 3:16)*

Jesus came to save us from sin and its penalty by paying the ultimate price in our place. No human could pay the penalty for another's sin because each of our lives are already forfeit in payment for our own sin. But if there were a person without sin, he could pay the penalty for someone else so that person could go to Heaven. Since Jesus is God, He had no sin. When He became a human, He was still without sin. Jesus is the only one who could die in our place, a substitute for our sin.

Since Jesus paid the penalty for our sin, God is able to offer us eternal life that we did not earn; "The gift of God is eternal life in Christ Jesus our Lord" (Romans 6:23). Since it is a gift, all we have to do is receive it. How do we receive this gift? The Bible tells us:

> *If you confess with your mouth the Lord Jesus and believe in your heart that God has raised Him from the dead, you will be saved. For with the heart one believes unto righteousness, and with the mouth confession is made unto salvation. (Romans 10:9–10)*

It is very simple.

1. Confess that you are a sinner and need a Savior to rescue you from sin and death;
2. Believe that Jesus is the Son of God, that He died for your sin, and that He was raised from the dead;
3. Ask Jesus to forgive your sins and apply His death in your place.

That's all it takes to have your sin forgiven, to gain a new life, and to begin a personal relationship with Jesus. Once you have done that, the messages in this book and the resources in Appendix B will help you grow in and enjoy your relationship with Him.

Also, let me know if this book helped you decide to trust Jesus, so I can pray for you. The *About the Author* page at the end tells how to connect with me.

Appendix B – Resources to Keep Listening

Remember, this book only looked at 30 messages from Heaven. However, the Bible is full of God's messages that address all areas of life, messages that you can apply each day. To keep listening, please make time to spend with the Bible every day. For help in learning and understanding what the Lord has said, check out these ministries that have blessed me.

The Bible Broadcasting Network – https://BBNRadio.org
   Commercial-free, high quality Christian programming for all ages and stages of life from great Bible teachers with wonderful music in between programs.

BBN Bible Institute – https://bbn1.bbnradio.org/bbnbienglish/
   A ministry of the Bible Broadcasting Network, it provides free online Bible audio classes.

Thru the Bible Radio – https://TTB.org
   Dr. J. Vernon McGee leads a five-year study through the entire Bible in 30-minute segments each weekday. There are also many Bible learning and study materials available.

God has given the local church to assist you spiritually. I highly recommend finding and attending a local church where they believe the Bible is the literal Word of God and take it seriously.

You may also like to go through my book *Seeking the Lord, A 30 Day Start to Your Journey.* It's designed to help people grow spiritually and learn about seeking God over a lifetime. Learn more at https://KeonLindsey.com.

About the Author

Keon Lindsey is a former Business Consultant, Project Management Professional, and Navy Veteran with a variety of life experiences. He has earned a Black Belt in American Freestyle Karate, worked for himself, flown small airplanes and large jets, and has a master's degree in Aeronautical Engineering.

Yet, what brings Keon lasting satisfaction is studying and sharing God's Word, the Bible. He is a life-long Bible student and has lead Bible studies for adults and teenagers. He lives with his family in Virginia and enjoys jogging and summer fruits. Keon hopes that his writings inspire you to seek true satisfaction as well.

His first book, *Seeking the Lord, a 30-Day Start to Your Journey* was published in 2020. It is a full-length Bible study devotional available on Amazon and would be a great next step after reading this book. Sign up for Keon's newsletter to stay informed about new book progress including:

Bad Boys of the Bible, A 30-Day Adventure

Book reviews on Amazon are really appreciated and helpful so others can discover and benefit from this book. Also, Keon welcomes questions and comments. You can connect with him on his website.

You can connect with me on:

🌐 https://keonlindsey.com

f https://www.facebook.com/KeonLindseyBooks

Also by Keon Lindsey

Seeking the Lord, A 30 Day Start to Your Journey examines true stories of how 22 people in the Bible searched for and found God. From Abraham to Rahab and Joseph to Jairus, both famous and little-known people demonstrate that you can know God and have a life worth remembering!

These timeless examples will help guide your journey of seeking. They are arranged in 30 chapters for daily reading. The goal is to provide a one-month jumpstart to your quest. This book will show that you can have a life filled with satisfaction even in our stressed and hectic times.

Seeking the Lord, A 30 Day Start to Your Journey
"If you want to gain a deeper understanding of how to seek the Lord, this book is a must." Reader's Favorite